THE NEW CONTEXTUAL THERAPY

THE NEW CONTEXTUAL THERAPY
Guiding the Power of Give and Take

by

Terry D. Hargrave, PhD
and
Franz Pfitzer, MD

BRUNNER-ROUTLEDGE

New York and Hove

Published in 2003 by
Brunner-Routledge
29 West 35th Street
New York, NY 10001
www.brunner-routledge.com

Published in Great Britain by
Brunner-Routledge
27 Church Road
Hove, East Sussex
BN3 2FA
www.brunner-routledge.co.uk

Brunner-Routledge is an imprint of the Taylor & Francis Group.
Printed in the United States of America on acid-free paper.

10 9 8 7 6 5 4 3 2 1

Library of Congress Cataloging-in-Publication Data

Hargrave, Terry D.
    The new contextual therapy : guiding the power of give and take / by
Terry D. Hargrave & Franz Pfitzer.
        p. ; cm.
    Includes bibliographical references and index.
    ISBN 0-415-93437-0 (hardback : alk. paper)
    1. Contextual therapy. 2. Family therapy. 3. Psychotherapy.
    [DNLM: 1. Psychotherapy. 2. Interpersonal Relations. 3. Professional
    Practice—ethics. WM 420 H279n 2003] I. Pfitzer, Franz. II. Title.

    RC488.55.H37 2003
    616.89'14—dc21

                                                    2003009523

To my siblings, Patricia Carol, Charley Bevard, and Gary Bryant

TERRY D. HARGRAVE, PHD

To my parents, Dr. Franz and Irmgard Pfitzer, and my wife,
Evelyn Seidel-Pfitzer—for teaching me love and trustworthiness.
To my children, Martin, Lara, Anna, and Lukas—
for being such a joy in my life.

FRANZ PFITZER, MD

Contents

Section II: The Techniques of Contextual Therapy

Preface

We, the authors, are from different countries, but we are very much related. We are bound together because we share a common lineage in our professional work through Ivan Boszormenyi-Nagy, MD. We are a psychiatrist and a psychotherapist who believe in the contextual therapy approach not only because we have seen it work with our patients, but also because it works in our own families.

Terry Hargrave is a psychotherapist who became acquainted with contextual therapy and Dr. Boszormenyi-Nagy while in graduate school in the mid-1980s. The approach was not only essential to his own growth and resolution of family issues, but it became a research and clinical interest. Hargrave spent time studying Boszormenyi-Nagy's writings and trained with him three times. Franz Pfitzer is a psychiatrist at the Klinik St. Irmingard in Prien, Germany. Pfitzer invited Dr. Boszormenyi-Nagy to lecture at the Klinik for many years in the 1990s, where his influence on the therapeutic community was profound. When Dr. Boszormenyi-Nagy ended his lectures, Franz invited Terry to lecture at the Klinik, starting in 1998 and continuing to the present. In this 5-year collaboration, we have found a great deal of common interest in contextual therapy, as well as a deep and enduring friendship.

We both agreed that the contextual approach was profound and offered a comprehensive theory integrating and balancing concerns of individuality and togetherness. We believed deeply in the psychotherapist's ability to use this approach to reshape human relationships using the strengths of trust, fairness, and freedom. We also observed, however, that the usefulness of the approach had gone unnoticed by many psychotherapists and mental health workers. One of the reasons for this lack of attention is that the theory was based in a philosophy and a language that were often hard to read and understand. We began discussions 3 years ago about the possibility of developing a "handbook" of contextual therapy that would be written in clearer language and that avoided getting bogged down in the philosophical underpinnings. Three years later, this book is the result.

Our desire for this text is that readers will be able to clearly grasp the four dimensions of relationships in the contextual approach and how these dimensions interact in the therapeutic process. Although we realize that the contextual approach is complex, we hope that this book will serve readers as a primer on the theory, enabling them to understand and apply this methodology. In order to accomplish this task, we have tried to "boil down" the essential elements in each dimension. Also, we have taken some new directions from the traditional contextual approach in seeking to explain the dimensions of individual psychology and relational ethics. Finally, we have tried to add more specifics and techniques to the therapeutic application and intervention of multidirected partiality. Of course, any time there is simplification, there is omission. We realize that ours will not be a definitive work on contextual therapy, and we have no desire for it to be so. Our desire is strictly to help students and clinicians more easily grasp the helpfulness of contextual therapy and learn how to mobilize change in a new manner.

Section I of the book focuses on the basics of the theory. We hope that this section will serve to demystify the theory. Chapters 3 and 5 are particularly crucial in this process. In chapter 3, we explain the essential elements of love and trust and how these constructs provide the foundation and the substance for individual personality and actions. We are proposing a simplified idea of how attachment, behavior, and constructivism interact to produce very complex behavior. In chapter 5 we take on the challenge of clarifying the workings and the effect of the dimension of relational ethics. Because this dimension has been rarely recognized in psychotherapy, contextual therapists in the past have found it necessary to create almost a new language of therapeutic process to accurately identify the impact. Although we do use some of this language, we have tried to keep unfamiliar terminology to a minimum and to explain the contextual terms using familiar therapy concepts.

Section II of the book is dedicated to illustrating how the contextual approach can be used in interventions. In the past, multidirected partiality has been identified as the primary technique in contextual therapy. We agree that multidirected partiality is the primary attitude and technique of the approach, but we try to specify how different techniques fit under the umbrella of this type of partiality. We hope that the reader will find the specifics a further explanation of how to utilize the approach effectively. We have broadly divided the techniques that promote change under two chapters. Chapter 6 deals with therapeutic techniques that are aimed at addressing the violations that individuals internalize. Chapter 7 discusses the efforts in therapy to correct and heal violations that are passed along in the form of generational damage. Both chapters essentially deal with healing violations of love and trust, but one is directed more toward the individual, whereas the other is more toward the family. Of course, both types of interventions are actually used in the process of change.

No such work is accomplished without the help and sacrifice of many. We wish to express our deep appreciation and affection to Ivan Boszormenyi-Nagy for his encouragement in our lives and his support of our work. Although we do have ideas that differ, we have always found him supportive of extending new ideas about contextual therapy. We also wish to thank our families for their understanding and sacrifice, as we worked to discuss, teach, and write about our ideas. Our wives and children have made these sacrifices of time with grace and have done us the great pleasure of also becoming friends with one another.

The Dimensions of Contextual Family Therapy

CHAPTER 1

The Basics of the Theory

Contextual family therapy is about understanding and intervening effectively in relationships. This is a description, more than a definition, of function. For years, students of therapy have been aware of the contextual family therapy approach as an important addition to the literature but usually are somewhat confused about the language, definition, and philosophy behind this type of therapy. It is as if people know that contextual therapy has something important and even profound to say about individuals and relationships, but they are not quite sure what that "something" is about. There are many reasons for this type of confusion, but a primary one is that the theory is so profound. It speaks about fair consideration, relational obligations, freedom, destructive entitlement, and loyalty. All of these concepts are not part of our everyday therapeutic language but carry hefty influence in the manner that individuals and relationships develop. The confusion, however, over the difficult language and the hard-to-understand philosophy usually translates into the profound concepts being little thought about and, more important, being little used.

This book attempts to change some of these problems. When we say *new* contextual therapy, we mean no disrespect to those who have written about the contextual approach in previous years. Indeed, the work of others in the contextual therapy arena has changed our lives and has certainly changed the way we do therapy. Neither is the term *new* meant to give the connotation that the approach that we describe in these pages is the definitive work about contextual therapy. When we say *new*, we mean that this book makes every effort to make the concepts of contextual therapy more accessible to the student of therapy and to the clinician interested in mastering the approach.

Our purpose here is to present the therapy in a clearer language and to underpin the concepts with clinical examples. Also, we hope to present some new formulations based on our clinical understanding of the dynamics of the therapy to move the contextual field forward. Some of these ideas do not hold with old conceptualizations of the theory and will move the reader outside the traditional understanding of contextual family therapy. Our intent, however, is not to try and reject the ideas of the past but to effectively build on them to provide the reader with a good primer on the subject of contextual therapy and to make the therapy usable and dynamic in a person's clinical work.

Furthermore, we write this book now because contextual family therapy is at a critical juncture. Without clarification, this essential theory is in danger of being recognized by the larger family therapy field in only a cursory manner or being ignored totally. In order for this helpful model to grow, it must have a wider acceptance in training programs that eventually produce contextual therapists.

WHY ARE THEORIES OR MODELS NECESSARY?

We currently see two dangerous trends in the field of psychotherapy. The first concerns the nature of the psychotherapeutic field. The whole endeavor of the psychological pursuit has been the scientific understanding of behavior and mental processes. We are in agreement with the intent of science in psychotherapy. Psychotherapy needs to be about using sound empirical methodologies to "prove" the efficacy and the successful clinical outcomes of practice. The current trend in the last decade, however, is to insist that unless good science and research back up everything we do or say clinically, then our clinical work is at best questionable and at worst unethical. Government and the insurance industry have added to this notion that if you cannot prove clinical outcomes by the techniques used, then the clinical practice is largely useless. This has certainly made the psychotherapy community more responsible in consideration of techniques and practice, but it has also had the undesirable effect of making the community more tentative. Most who are in some type of psychotherapeutic work have a tendency to stick to the "book" of proven methodology and are hesitant to develop truly new ideas and techniques. In the field of family therapy, for instance, there was a time period in the 1960s and 1970s when new ideas and theories flourished. Yet in the last decade, very few "new" ideas have been developed and no new major theoretical perspectives presented. Although ideas of science and clinical efficacy are good, when taken to the extreme, they have resulted in the stagnation of therapeutic technique.

The second trend that concerns us is somewhat an outgrowth of the first. As individuals in the psychotherapeutic community are forced to "prove" their work, they become primarily interested in specific techniques. Instead of having a broad understanding of the complexity of human nature and the intricacies necessary to encourage change, many psychotherapists have become "technique junkies" (Hargrave & Anderson, 1992). In doing so, there is a performance of practice instead of sensitivity to need. It is similar to a person knowing one chord or a set of chords on a musical instrument. He or she may know how to play one note or one song but certainly does not know how to play or to be a master of the instrument. In order to really play or master the music, one must have an understanding of the dynamics and the unique character of the instrument and how it fits within the larger scheme of orchestration (Hargrave & Anderson, 1992). Without this understanding, psychotherapists become more or less assembly-line workers, turning out patients on whom they have performed the specified technique.

Psychotherapy is and should be based on good science, because science employs the empirical methodology necessary to lead us to what is true and what works. But in addition, we also believe that psychotherapy is an art. Art also pursues truth, but it uses a different methodology. Art's methodology is aimed at expression, emotion, and perspective. Psychotherapy must always struggle to balance itself in this precarious position, striving for scientific investigation to legitimize practice and acknowledging that much of what is done in psychotherapy is about how therapists use themselves in an emotional and beautiful way to bring about change. When the psychotherapeutic community becomes imbalanced to either side of science or art, then the result will ultimately be irresponsibility or stagnation. Theories or models provide a guide for the psychotherapist on how to perform this difficult balancing act. Theoretical perspective gives broad understanding not only of the psychotherapist but also about human nature, change, and development. It provides the beginning point for people to express their ideas and allows them to apply perspective to the human condition. But good theory also provides the constructs necessary for testing and falsification. Science is therefore used to inform the theory about how the ideas and the perspective work in reality. This should, in turn, lead the psychotherapist into better-informed artistic expression in clinical work. Good theory should give the psychotherapist an opportunity to produce synergy, as art and science both inform one another in the pursuit of truth.

Good theory also enables psychotherapists to organize not only their techniques but also their therapeutic talents. Instead of psychotherapists randomly using this or that technique, they have a theoretical organization that provides appropriate direction and understanding for when and how to use techniques. In addition, theory allows psychotherapists to understand how they best use the human expression of emotion and perspective to help patients who are in distress. To allude to the musical metaphor, theory gives the psychotherapist a musical score in which to refer, organize, and judge the performance of clinical work.

Contextual family therapy offers another dimension of theory that is unique to therapy. Not only does it help organize psychotherapists' talents and offer a basis for diagnostics and assessment, it also provides ethical targets for the therapy. One of the foundations of this theory is to give due consideration to clients, their development, and how previous relationships have shaped their thoughts, emotions, and behavior. Just as important, however, is that the theory also considers how the actions, emotions, and thoughts of the individual have affected and will affect the person's current relationships and the relationships of generations to come.

Contextual family therapy is a very good model for clinical practice because it is an integrative theoretical approach. As pointed out by others (Gurman & Kniskern, 1981), it is almost a compilation of approaches or a "theory of theories." As such, contextual family therapy gives psychotherapists the opportunity to organize their perspective on the human condition, as well as to put meaning to the techniques of clinical practice.

INTRODUCTION TO CONTEXTUAL THERAPY

Life is relational. It is difficult to imagine any kind of learning, sense of self, or understanding of the world without relationships. The philosopher/theologian Martin Buber (1958) put forth these thoughts in his articulation of the idea of *I and Thou*. The basic idea behind Buber's work is that without another person reflecting back to me interpretations about ideas, actions, and physical being, there is no effective way for me to understand what I think, what I do, and how I look. At a very simple level, for instance, there is no way for me to construct the idea that my hair is combed in a pleasing way unless I get or have gotten the feedback from others that my hair does indeed look good. I cannot construct this idea in a vacuum in my head. It is dependent upon my relating to the environment and to people around me. The environment and other people give me the action context needed to interpret the necessary concepts of self and worthwhile activities. It is my relationship with the environment and with people that gives me the ability to know anything. In order to understand *I,* therefore, I must be in context with *Thou.*

This simple, yet profound, concept gives us the ability to say that there is a relational imperative about life. Even if I give up on mankind and move to a deserted island, the conceptions that I have had in my past relationships with people will make up the necessary components of my self-understanding. Relationships with others serve as the basis for our understanding of ourselves, just as the relationships others have with us serve as the basis for their understanding of themselves. It is the relationship, therefore, that is essential to understand because it forms the basis of not only how people interact but also who they perceive themselves to be.

Because the contextual family therapy approach is integrative, the foundation is built on the idea that relationships are based on and influenced by four dimensions of reality. These dimensions are facts, individual psychology, systemic interactions, and relational ethics (Boszormenyi-Nagy & Ulrich, 1981). These four dimensions can be discussed separately for the purposes of teaching and articulation, but it is important to realize that they are always intertwined and inseparable in the effect of and work in relationships. The four dimensions always mutually affect one another and the relational field; the whole of the dimensions is greater than the sum of the parts (Hargrave & Anderson, 1992).

Facts

This first dimension is essentially about the facts about life and the relationship that are true but are difficult to change. It includes factors such as our genetic input, physical health, basic history, and events in our life cycles (Boszormenyi-Nagy & Krasner, 1986). We can easily see how this dimension plays into relationships. For instance, if a person is diabetic, he or she has to constantly be aware of how the condition will affect health. Diet, medication, and lifestyle are all affected by the disease. In addition, the people who relate to the diabetic are impacted by how the person manages life. One can see how a husband who is diabetic and is in deteriorating health and refuses to take care of himself might lead his wife to want to become overinvolved or even nagging in the relationship, in an effort to improve his condition. The factual condition would perhaps affect the relationship by producing fear, depression, resentment, and anger and might be the primary focus of interactions.

It is important to realize that the dimension of facts is objectifiable. In other words, there is a way to know, touch, or feel contact with this dimensional reality. We may not be able to discover all the facts that exist and affect relationships, but it does not change the reality that the facts *can* be discovered. For instance, people may not inform others that they come from a divorced family and may not believe that the divorce affected them in the least. However, the choice the parents made to divorce makes up a factual history for individuals that they cannot change and most likely affects, even if unconsciously, how they eventually interact with others. All facts—appearance, socio-economic history, circumstances, and life choices, just to name a few—affect this first dimension and involve a dynamic interaction in relationships. The therapeutic conceptualization and effort in this dimension are described in the next chapter.

Individual Psychology

This dimension relates to how the individual took the information given in the external environment and in relationships and then internalized this into cognitive information concerning beliefs, experiences, emotions, feelings, volitions, motivations, and memories. It basically describes the process of how individuals develop traits that strive for love, power, and pleasure (Boszormenyi-Nagy & Krasner, 1986). In the past, contextual family therapy has been heavily influenced to describe this dimension in psychoanalytic terms. Fairbairn's (1963) object relations approach is especially noteworthy, as is Erickson's (1963) work in describing the psychosocial stages. In chapter 3, we present a different understanding of the underpinnings of individual psychology for clinical application. But no matter what the methodology of describing the process, this dimension concerns the process in which individuals eventually develop ideas about themselves and move toward expressing those ideas in action, which we eventually call *personality*.

As opposed to the first dimension of facts, the dimension of individual psychology is subjective in nature. In other words, we can never be quite sure about the dynamics and actions that lead an individual to construct certain ideas, beliefs, or motivations for behavior. Two individuals who come from the same genetic background and have very similar experiences may construct very different individual psychologies. This subjective fact of construction means that we can never articulate with absolute certainty the way an individual's beliefs, motivations, and emotions are developed and will continue to change through the developmental life course.

Systemic Interactions

Simply stated, the third dimension of systemic interactions deals with the communication patterns in relationships. Our knowledge about this dimension is actually based on general systems theory and cybernetics (Goldenberg & Goldenberg, 2000) and puts forth the idea that the behavioral interactions of the *supraindividual level* constitute an entity of their own. This entity, or system, produces transactions that regulate and define the system that we can see in the way of organizational structure, power alignments, and common system beliefs. For example, if a family comes into therapy and a parent consistently dominates the conversation with the therapist, defining the problem and the efforts of the family to improve the situation, we could easily see that the parent holds most of the power, which creates a structure where he or she is in control of the family, which in turn produces a belief that perhaps that parent will not listen or that no one else in the family has anything important to say. Also, symptoms or dysfunctions may be interactions that actually maintain the system. For instance, if a father is depressed over his unhappy marriage, a son—either consciously or unconsciously—may start acting out in some fashion. If the son fails in school or engages in some delinquent activity, the father has to focus his attention on dealing with the son. This interaction by the son accomplishes competency with the father, as the parent must move past the depression in order to be a "good parent." Thus, the symptomology of the son maintains the father's functioning and preserves the system (Hargrave & Anderson, 1992).

The third dimension is also objectifiable, meaning that we can see or articulate the interactions and transactions that take place within relationships. Although postmodern therapists have been particularly critical of systems thinking, believing that the concept leads psychotherapists to assume that they can objectively diagnose relationships (White, 1995) or that the concepts of rules and homeostasis are actually constructs that exist in relationship (deShazer, 1991), there are undeniable patterns and transactions in relationships that can be predicted. Whether or not these patterns are system rules or simple constructed choices, they are still objectifiable transactions that impact the interactions in relationships. The important point of this dimension, therefore, is that relational transactions become predictable for members in relationships and therefore lead to beliefs and actions around power and organization. Although contextual therapists are most often thought of as psychodynamic or family-of-origin theorists, the third dimension offers many opportunities for interventions. The contextual understanding of this dimension and an integrative approach to interventions are discussed in chapter 4.

Relational Ethics

The three previous dimensions of relationships are familiar to the psychotherapeutic community and have been well practiced for many years. It is the fourth dimension of relational ethics that sets the contextual family therapy approach apart and offers new understanding to the therapeutic field. Relational ethics deal with the balance of what people give in relationships, as opposed to what they merit or are entitled to get from others. As relational members interact in the balance of give-and-take, relational ethics require them to assume responsibility for actions and, it is hoped, build the relational resource of trustworthiness (Hargrave, Jennings, & Anderson, 1991). The welfare and the interests of every relational member are taken into account by others, and individuals strive for the balance of fairness between what each member is obligated to give and entitled to receive. These patterns and balances in the relational ethics dimension, however, do not impact the relational members only in the present time. The patterns and balances and the trustworthiness are passed from one generation to the next and serve as the keys to understanding individual and family functioning (Goldenberg & Goldenberg, 2000).

Although it is acknowledged that the dimensions are inseparable, it is clear that Boszormenyi-Nagy and Krasner (1986) consider the relational ethics dimension to be the most powerful and influential in shaping relationships. Symptoms appear when relational imbalances and violations of trustworthiness occur (Boszormenyi-Nagy, Grunebaum, & Ulrich, 1991). Contextual therapists believe that most powerful healing factors that can be mobilized in psychotherapy are in this dimension.

Of course, this dimension is by nature subjective. Although we can attempt to articulate the mechanisms of give-and-take, the perceptions of giving, balance, fairness, and entitlement are all constructed among the relational members. This does not mean that the subjective nature of the dimension makes its effects in either strengthening or weakening relationships less real. These subjective forces of love and trustworthiness are powerful, not only in shaping individual perceptions of self, but also in producing interactions that are common from one generation to the next. This important dimension in the contextual approach is explained in detail in chapter 5.

THE INTERACTION OF THE RELATIONAL DIMENSIONS

Partly because of the novelty of the fourth dimension to psychotherapy and partly because of the emphasis given to the dimension by the founders, relational ethics have been the focus of contextual therapy (Boszormenyi-Nagy & Krasner, 1986). Relational ethics have been described as an "umbrella" over the other dimensions or "the heavy door" through which understanding is essential but difficult.

There is no doubt that relational ethics are the important foundation of contextual therapy; however, all the dimensions are dynamic and interactive in a mutually supportive function. The four dimensions, therefore, are mutually dependent upon one another. This fact makes it difficult to articulate one dimension as being more powerful than the others.

The important points of the interactions between the dimensions lie in the subjective and objective natures of each. Facts and systemic interactions are both objective in nature, whereas individual psychology and relational ethics are subjective in nature. A simple way to think about this is that facts and systemic interactions are what we can see or articulate by the nature of information or observation, whereas individual psychology and relational ethics are what we can't see and we depend on being reflected through interpretation, perception, and feeling. Again, it is important to emphasize that just because the latter two dimensions are not objectifiable, they are nonetheless real in their effect on individuals and relationships.

As illustrated in figure 1.1, the facts and the systemic interactions are the medium in which information is communicated or taken in by the individual. For instance, a child who is born with good health and to parents from a middle-income socioeconomic background is experiencing the objective dimension of facts. The parents love the child, but they want the child to behave more like an adult than like a child. As the child grows in years, the parents increasingly depend on the child emotionally to stay with them and make them feel loved and wanted. The child, not knowing any different, will attempt to fill the parents' request. But, as often is the case, the child will fail because he or she is not mature enough to emotionally take care of an adult. As the parents' frustration with the child grows, they may make com-

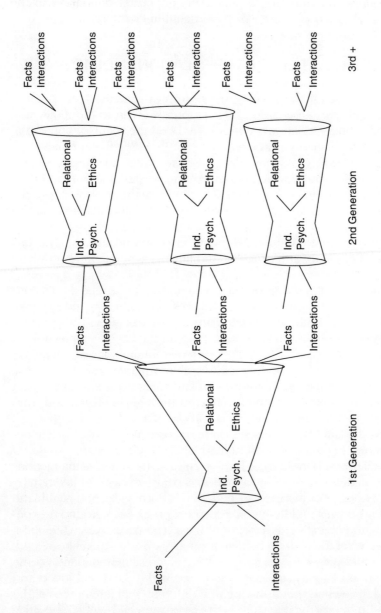

FIGURE 1.1. Interactions of the Contextual Therapy Dimensions

ments such as, "We do so much for you and you can't even show us that you care," or "Can't you do anything right?" These types of communications and transactions are in the objectifiable dimension of systemic interaction. The objective communications are the only way we learn about relationships.

These objective dimensions are taken in by children and they begin to construct ideas about themselves and how they have to interact with the environment. These ideas or beliefs are cognitively constructed, but the ideas focus on how the child decides to interact with the environment and on the sense of self the child develops. For example, children in this illustration may carry the feeling that something is deeply wrong with them because the parents aren't quite sure that the children measure up. The children may also come to the conclusion that because they fail the parents, it is best to avoid relationships and relating whenever possible. These constructions are the subjective work of the dimension of individual psychology illustrated in figure 1.1 as the internal part of the megaphone. As children grow into adults, they will increasingly be put in situations that require them to relate at a more vigorous level. They begin to conceptualize an evaluation of how good or bad their parents were at parenting. They feel the drive to answer deep questions concerning self. Did they measure up? Didn't they deserve better treatment? Weren't they cheated out of the opportunity for a normal childhood? Couple this with the fact that the now adult children are likely still interacting with the parents in a similar fashion: The parents may still be critical of how the children emotionally connect with them, while at the same time be dependent on the adult children to get emotional security. As the adult children move into the developmental years of perhaps seeking a mate or having children of their own, critical formations and decisions are being made, both consciously and unconsciously, concerning the nature of relationships and what they are entitled to receive and obligated to give. These constructions now deal with the subjective dimension of relational ethics.

As figure 1.1 illustrates, however, relational ethics take form in the objective world through how these adults now influence the factual dimension and interact through other relationships. In other words, the formation of the individual psychology and relational ethics in the subjective frame will now be expressed through the factual and systemic interactive dimensions of the objective frame. Take notice, however, that as the information moves from the relational ethics dimension into the objective world, it spreads out to multiple relationships. Because relational ethics influence behavior and belief in so many relationships, the process resembles the large end of the megaphone, giving amplification to the internal constructs. As these adults influence and interact with multiple people, including friends, spouses, and children, the ethical base that they developed plays out in many relationships. These influences and interactions (facts and systemic interactions) now form the makings of what others in the second generation of relationships will use to form their own individual psychologies and their legacy of how to relate in the ethical dimension. It is likely, using our previous example, that the adults will have the expectation that their spouses or children should make efforts to take care of them emotionally, just as they made a good-faith effort to care for their parents. They will likely feel entitled to preferential treatment because they are looking for approval and acceptance that were not received from their parents. Finally, they may become critical when their relationships do not meet their needs. Of course, all of these decisions and interactions are used by people in the second generation of relationships to develop constructions about individual psychologies and relational ethics. In turn, these people will influence and interact with others, based on their ideas about themselves and the relational ethics they have developed. The dynamics will be passed from the second generation to the third, the third to the fourth generation, and so forth.

The dimension of relational ethics is so powerful because of this passing from one generation to the next. With each generation comes more relationships. If there is a constructive relational ethic that is healthy and responsible, this will be reproduced in multiple relationships. If the ethic is destructive, however, each person who inherited the formation of the relational ethic will feel entitled to get from the future generation what he or she did not get from the past. So the dimension of relational ethics is not exactly an umbrella over interactions with the other dimensions. Rather, we see this dimension's power lies in the way it amplifies what occurs in the other dimensions, which is then passed along to future relationships and generations.

CHAPTER 2

Just the Facts

So much of what affects relationships and even the psychology of individuals consists of simple facts. Some of these facts may change, as experience and interaction proceed—for example, in the case of a temporary financial setback or a serious illness that can be cured. But for the most part, facts are realities that cannot be changed and that the individual or the family must live with forever. A partial list of these would include early deaths of family members, malnutrition, child abuse, genetic heritage, disabilities, adoption, and school performance (Boszormenyi-Nagy & Krasner, 1986). We have no control over these realities, but they affect who we are as individuals and how we engage in relationships.

Certainly, these facts require attention from the psychotherapist, apart from the individual or the family reaction to them (Boszormenyi-Nagy & Krasner, 1986). In many cases, simply addressing the factual situations that allow change can make a tremendous difference in the functioning of people and their relationships. For instance, a woman initiates therapy with her 72-year-old mother. The mother has been chronically anxious and overdependent upon the daughter for years but has recently become so anxious that she calls for her daughter's help between 10 and 20 times a day. The daughter's anger is tremendous because she simply sees the mother's actions as more of the same unpleasant behavior that has existed since childhood. When the psychotherapist, however, discovers that the mother has not been eating correctly and has been misusing her medications, a factual reason for the increase in anxiety opens new opportunities for treatment. When the mother's nutritional needs are met and her medication issues are corrected, the behavior and the reactions, the frequency and the intensity of her anxiety, and her requests for attention subside. This not only solves an immediate problem for the mother and daughter, it gives them both the opportunity to address deeper emotional issues without the burden of these complicating problems.

There is a tendency for Western societies to overfocus on the factual dimension. It is as if many say, "If only this fact were different in my life, then my problems would be solved." For instance, if the person had more money, didn't have diabetes, were left alone by children or parents, or had more education, life would improve. Sometimes these changes are possible and sometimes not. The reality is, however, that people have a tendency to fantasize about the factual dimension changing, or they try too hard to effect changes in these realities, and it consumes much of the energy that they have to address issues. Many times this focus distracts individuals from facing deeper psychological or relational issues that also need attention.

Most of the factual issues that can be easily addressed and changed are almost always dealt with by individuals long before they present themselves in therapy. Others that can be addressed with the psychotherapist's help often seem obvious. There are, however, three factual issues that often present themselves in therapy that can dominate the work or stagnate the progress in therapy. These issues concern biology, racial and ethnic background, and economic realities. Certainly, these three are not the only factual concerns, nor do they dominate all psychotherapy sessions, but they present themselves often and with enough intensity as to skew a patient's perspective or relationships. We believe, therefore, that it is the therapist's job to effectively address these three factual issues, in order to utilize the possible strengths that exist or to neutralize the negative effects that would possibly nullify therapy.

FACTUAL BIOLOGICAL CONCERNS FOR PSYCHOTHERAPISTS

There has been a debate in psychology from almost the inception of the field concerning the influences of heredity and environment on individual development and behavior (Himelstein, Graham, & Weinter, 1991). The course of this debate has taken different forms, but there seems to be an almost oscillating cycle of which side of the debate has the upper hand in explaining human behavior. The pendulum has definitely swung in the direction of heredity and genetic predisposition in the last decade. Much of this has been brought on by growing interest in the human genome. For instance, the Human Genome Project, which began in 1990 with the ambitious goal of mapping and identifying the genes in human DNA, planned to complete the project in 2005 (Human Genome Program, U.S. Department of Energy, *Genomics and Its Impact on Medicine and Society: A 2001 Primer,* 2001). A completed draft of the entire human genome sequence was announced in 2000, which put the project well ahead of schedule. The astounding discoveries of the project have had dramatic implications. For instance, there are 30,000 to 35,000 genes, far less than what was predicted. Over 99% of genetic information is the same for all people, and over 50% of the genes have a function that is yet to be discovered. But the draft has also revealed new information about genes that are associated with disease. Links between genes have been associated with breast cancer, muscle disease, deafness, and blindness. In addition, DNA sequences are thought to be the underlying cause of common diseases such as cardiovascular disease, diabetes, arthritis, and many forms of cancer. Along with the genetic map having an enormous impact on molecular medicine, it has also had a dramatic impact on how mutations in genes have progressed through evolution over the course of history (Li, Gu, Wang & Nekrutenko, 2001).

With these kinds of findings from just one of the many investigations into human genetics, it is easy to understand why many people believe that human beings are "hardwired" to behave and think the way that they do because of their genetic heritage (Baltimore, 2001). Many believe that it is just a matter of time before the breadth of human physiology, development, and evolution as well as of cognitive function, emotional well-being, and behavior, are at least associated with, if not caused by, genetics.

These are indeed exciting times in the field of biology. The genetic discoveries are only beginning, and at times, it does seem as if all of our thoughts and behaviors will eventually be associated with our genetic heritage. But it is clear over the course of psychological investigation that both heredity and environment play important roles in the development and behavior of humans and that different aspects of this development and behavior are influenced more by heredity and others influenced more by environment (Coll, 1990). It is even more complex, however, from a contextual therapy perspective. As seen in figure 2.1, even if we start with the notion that genetic predisposition is the initiator of development and behavior [Facts (1)], it quickly interacts with the environment and with our experiences [Environment (1) and Experience (1)]. As the individual proceeds through development with time, the previous realities of facts, experience, and environment interact with new facts, experiences, and environments [Facts (2), Experience (2), and Environment (2)]. The progression of time leads us to have a constant interaction not only

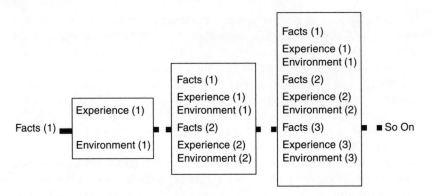

FIGURE 2.1. The Interaction of Facts, Experience, and Environment

between our factual predeterminants, environmental situations, and behavioral experiences but also with all the facts, situations, and behaviors that have preceded. This historical accumulation of who we are and the way we affect others becomes more and more diffuse in terms of determining which interactions are the most important and to what extent each dimension affects the others. The result is that science will never fully separate the impact of biological and environmental forces in absolutely determining "causes" for physiology, development, and behavior. No doubt, there are genetic influences for some psychological disorders, such as mood disorders (Tsuang & Faraone, 1990), schizophrenia (Prescott & Gottesman, 1993), and anxiety (Torgersen, 1990). The way and to what degree, however, these genetic influences interact with environmental, experiential, and historical interactions of the dimensions in the past are far from being determined.

Therefore, it is necessary for the psychotherapist to take a pragmatic approach to the factual history of a patient. The patient may want to know the reasons for "the way I am" or "why I behave as I do," but for the most part, we cannot separate these facts from the confusion of life. Many patients have a tendency to point toward these facts as excuses for either not working on problems or working on fruitless pursuits to solve problems. For example, the following is from a therapy session with a 39-year-old woman who was seeking help for her depression.

Woman: I have been depressed for so long, I really can't remember what it's like to feel any different. I think that I'm just one

of those people who is prone to depression—you know—
I have a chemical imbalance.

Therapist: That may well be true. Many people do have a brain chemistry that works against them when it comes to depression. But if that is the fact, what can we do here to make your life better?

Woman: You can make me not depressed. I certainly can't make myself.

Therapist: Of course, I can't make you "undepressed" either. We can, however, accept the fact that you do have some depression and can find ways to understand who you are and maybe help.

Woman: I don't know. I keep telling my husband that it's his fault. He had an affair a few years ago and I have never really recovered from it. I tell him every now and again when he wants me to feel better that it's his fault that I feel awful in the first place. I just really don't see any way that I can make progress.

Although it is easy to understand that this woman is in much pain and she has formulated an identity around depression to express her unhappiness about her husband's infidelity, she uses her physiological brain chemistry and her husband's actions as reasons that she cannot make progress in therapy. In cases such as these, it is necessary for the psychotherapist to help patients not only accept the facts as they are but use those facts for a basis for learning more about themselves. This is done by the psychotherapist in the previous case, later in the same session.

Therapist: I can see how there are factors that work against you in overcoming this depression. I can also see that you have some good reasons to be depressed. (Long silence)

Woman: Yeah. I'm not sure what to do, but I know that I have to do something.

Therapist: In some ways, depression can make you aware of how necessary it is to have hope that things can get better. When were not depressed, we take our mood for granted because we almost always can find something that is positive. Depression reminds us not to take hopefulness in life for granted.

Woman: That's for sure. I want to have hope again.

Therapist: Then we must use your depression to point the way to
            hope. It will tell you the things that are most painful about
            life and also show you the areas where you are so strong
            that it can't throw you off track.

Woman: I've never looked at it that way, but I see where you are
            right. No matter how depressed I've been, I've always been
            able to respond to my friends. They enjoy me and I do
            enjoy them.

Therapist: Then that is a strength that your depression has revealed.
            You can learn from that strength to help you live with the
            fact that you are depressed.

Woman: I would like to learn more about that.

Not only does the psychotherapist help the woman accept the
fact that she is depressed, the therapist begins to move the woman to
the point where she sees that the depression need not ruin every part
of her life. Indeed, the psychotherapist gives the woman a reason to
embrace the depression because it reveals some of her strengths. No
matter what the factual background is, from a genetic or environmental perspective, our job as psychotherapists must be to consider the
facts that have shaped the individual. When those facts are change-
able, we should assist the patient in making those changes. When,
however, those facts are stable and sometimes unchangeable, we must
help the patient accept the facts as they are and to embrace these as
having something to teach about life and relationships.

The other pressing biological issue in psychotherapy is the manipulation of the central nervous system by the use of psychotropic
drugs. Since the 1950s and 1960s, medication development for the
purpose of treating psychological disorders has increased and improved dramatically. Particularly, the last 15 years have seen phe-
nomenal growth in more efficient psychotropic medications that have
far less side effects than in the past. The problem, however, with
these medications is that much is still unknown about brain function
and why these medications work with some patients and not with
others. For both the psychotherapist and the patient, the question
becomes whether or not it is wise to use these types of medications.
Although there are various reasons for making decisions, people usually resist pharmacological treatment of psychological issues for one
of three reasons. First, people are often afraid of the consequences of
taking psychotropic medications, worrying that these will shorten or
lessen the quality of their lives. There are often reports of how ap-
proved drugs, once assumed to be safe, cause physical damage that

shows up only years after the drug was taken. Second, some people have a legitimate fear that if they take a drug that alters the brain, the substance will become addictive, similar to cocaine or alcohol. These people realize that physiological and psychological dependency on any substance ruins lives and relationships, and they feel that psychotropic medications might leave them addicted. Finally, some people simply fear that psychotropic medications will blunt the sensations or the thinking necessary to deal with or solve problems. If the pain or the problem is numbed by medication, then one is not really solving one's issue or getting the benefit of knowing what needs to change.

The issue of using psychotropic medication is extensively debated by both patients and helping professionals. Caution is called for, but the pragmatic approach is also necessary in this area. Because the detrimental side effects of medications have been curbed significantly in the last decade, it is much more reasonable to look at the potential benefits of psychotropics, compared to their potential risks. The risk of damage to the patient is far less now than with any previous generation of drugs. In addition, very few of these medications have addictive possibilities. To address the fear of avoiding one's problems, we see current medications simply as treating symptoms that may make it difficult for people to deal with certain problems or situations. Taking a medication for depression will not solve all emotional issues or situations, but the medication may make it possible for the patient to have enough energy to take steps to address an emotional issue. This class of medications, for the most part, has the possibility of "re-wiring" the patient's brain chemistry so that he or she has a more effective chance to deal with issues and problems in therapy. Medication is certainly not for every patient, and there are legitimate reasons to avoid these types of medications. There are also, however, many situations where the use of psychotropics can enhance therapy.

FACTUAL MULTICULTURAL CONCERNS FOR PSYCHOTHERAPISTS

Race, culture, and ethnicity are very hard to separate in reality. When we use the term *multiculturalism*, we agree with Pedersen (1990) that it includes factors such as demography (age, gender, place of residence), ethnography (ethnicity, nationality, religion, language usage), status (social, economic, and educational factors), and affiliations (formal memberships, informal networks). The primary emphasis in multicultural counseling for many years has been to manage and eliminate the fact that most psychotherapy has developed from a Western perspective and that it has a tendency to judge non-Western perspectives as dysfunctional or bad (Sue, Ivey, & Pedersen, 1996). The work to eliminate this bias is much needed. Psychotherapists consistently need to be aware of how their differences—be these racial, ethnic, religious, or sexual orientation—not only are a factual dimension that affects the helping relationship but also are factual inputs that have dramatically shaped patients.

Although there are many practical concerns in this area, we choose to focus on two issues in particular that many contextual psychotherapists manage with only great difficulty. These are issues of power differential and of historical multicultural issues of exploitation. The power differential that exists between many multicultural groups is obvious. It may stem from the fact that one is from a higher socioeconomic group, has more education, or is in the majority ethnic class. These differences are obvious but are especially complicating to the therapeutic relationship when the psychotherapist is in the more powerful position. This is further complicated by the fact that many patients, when they come to therapy, see themselves as "sick" and in need of being "cured." Because the psychotherapist is the helper, this gives him or her a more powerful position. Any time there is a power differential between psychotherapist and patient, a power struggle *will* ensue. Most of the time this struggle is covert, but it is nonetheless complicating to therapeutic relationships. The heart of the struggle is at the metacommunication of the patient improving. Whenever there are problems with improvement, patients are likely to feel less power in relation to the psychotherapist and they are likely to feel that the helper does not understand their problems. Patients will most often express this in the form of anger toward the psychotherapist or hopelessness toward their situation and their inability to make changes. The psychotherapist, on the other hand, is likely to feel this power differential in not being able to understand why patients cannot make improvements. "I have given the patient directives and support. What else does this individual need to make the necessary changes?" The psychotherapist will most often express these feelings through frustration or a desire to give up.

In power struggles concerning the progression of therapy, the key is not to eliminate them but rather to neutralize the effects that already exist. This is most effectively done through admission of the differential, by opening oneself to being taught from the other's perspective, and by the psychotherapist maintaining a one-down position in the therapeutic relationship. Observe how the following female therapist skillfully accomplishes this in working with a middle-aged black man who was struggling with controlling his anger.

Therapist: Now that I know a bit about what brings you to therapy, I would like to spend a short time talking about our relationship.

Man: What do you mean?

Therapist: We come from a very different perspective. I am female and you are male. I am white and you are black. We come from different family backgrounds, and I'm the counselor, wheras you are the client.

Man: I don't suppose you can understand what it's like to be a black man in this society, any more than I can understand what it's like to be a woman.

Therapist: You are right. We can never really fully understand one another. But I do want to learn more. I also want to be aware of any time I'm asking you to do something that feels demanding or insensitive.

Man: (Laughs) That may be most of the time.

Therapist: Did I already say something that made you feel angry or hopeless?

Man: (Long pause) Many white people say they want to understand and want to be sensitive. But when it gets down to it, they just give lip service to it.

Therapist: How can you help me avoid that position?

Man: (Looks at the therapist a long time in silence.) I will tell you when I feel that "white" coming out of you at me.

Because the therapist acknowledges the fact of the power differential, she exposes the man's feeling about her as a person and about the therapy in general. After the therapist puts herself in a one-down position, the man decides that he will be honest with her when he feels that she is taking the power position.

The second issue involves multicultural exploitation, and it grows out of generations of certain races having exploitive power over other. Examples of this type of exploitation are, unfortunately, not hard to find. It is of historical significance because the exploitation has not only served to form part of the identity of people who have suffered, it has also severely damaged the trustworthiness that exists in dimension four between different groups. When this type of exploitation exists between psychotherapist and patient, it is not enough for the helping professional to give admission. The psychotherapist must also acknowledge his or her responsibility in the exploitation.

As contextual therapists, we believe that trustworthiness does not simply exist in current relationships, but, rather, trustworthiness has either been built throught or has damaged previous generations of relationships. As a white man living in the 21st century, I may say that I have no responsibility for the persecution of blacks through the slavery of the 18th and 19th centuries. But the fact is, my white predecessors stole black people's freedom, heritage, and identity and passed the benefits they received from that exploitation down to the next generation. Even if those direct benefits diminished over the years, each generation in my lineage gained at least some advantages in life at the expense of the blacks who were exploited. In the same way, blacks in the 21st century have inherited the disadvantage of this exploitation throughout their generations. Is there any real way that whites can believe that the effects of slavery have not worked as a disadvantage to blacks living today? We do not think so. In the same vein, there is little alternative to the fact that whites living today have benefited from and have advantages over the black race that has been exploited.

The exploitation that exists between whites and blacks is only one example of the multicultural damage that has taken place in history. When this fact of past or current exploitation exists in a therapeutic relationship, the psychotherapist should admit not only that damage has been done but that he or she has some responsibility for the insults that have been delivered on behalf of previous generations. Sometimes this acknowledgment of responsibility will come in the form of an apology. Sometimes it may come in the form of an offer of reduced fees or of community service. The acknowledgment, however, is a trustworthy effort that affects the fourth dimension of relational ethics, which in turn has the potential of neutralizing the facts of the damaging past in the current therapeutic relationship.

FACTUAL ECONOMIC CONCERNS FOR PSYCHOTHERAPISTS

Although socioeconomic concerns are part of larger multicultural issues, they deserve special attention here. The factual dimension of how we in Western societies deal with economic realities has much predictive value in how both psychotherapists and patients view responsibility and change. It can be argued that in Western cultures,

TABLE 2.1
Positive and Negative Values Stemming From Economic Values

	CAPITALISM		COLLECTIVISM		
	Haves	Have Nots	Givers	Takers	
P O S I T I V E	Benefit Enjoyment Responsible	Opportunity-Seeking Competitive	Conscientious Social-Championing	Grateful Hard-Working	P O S I T I V E
N E G A T I V E	Indulgent Selfish	Envious Lazy	Pessimistic Resentful	Angry Entitled	N E G A T I V E

nothing brings about change and reorganization in relationships more powerfully than does economic stress. Table 2.1 illustrates an easy way to conceptualize differences in how people view economic realities.

As seen in the table, both capitalistic and collectivist economies have positives and negatives. Because capitalistic societies are competition-based, the positive values that are seen in people come from their ability to seek and enjoy opportunities for achievement. This system, however, has inherent flaws, in that the "haves" of society can drift into selfish and indulgent attitudes after they achieve a certain level of success and benefits. The "have nots" in a capitalistic environment may drift into being envious of those who have more but may be unwilling to take the necessary steps to actualize the opportunities. Collectivist societies, on the other hand, are based on cooperative care. When this system works, those who are able to give (givers) have the positive awareness of the community as a whole and seek to give to the social good. Those who are in need (takers) are grateful for the benefit they receive and do whatever they can to contribute to society. This system also has negative flaws, in that it is very possible that the givers of the society will resent being "used" by the system and may grow pessimistic concerning things ever effectively changing. The takers in these collectivist societies, on the other hand, may feel that they are entitled to the care of the social system and may turn to destructive anger to achieve these ends.

How does this relate to psychotherapy? There is, of course, a concern that the psychotherapist and the patient may come from divergent economic systems. Capitalistic ideas of competition and goal setting do not make much sense to a collectivist who is aiming for cooperation and taking good care of relationships. But there is also substantial concern around the issue of positive and negative relationships that develops around the facts of one's economic background. Because economic issues weigh so heavily in Western societies, there is a dominant perspective, although it is sometimes subtle, on how the system—and, particularly, people in the system—are viewed. For instance, if a psychotherapist comes from a capitalistic perspective but exhibits the negative traits of indulgence and selfishness, this systemically affects the patient who also comes from a capitalistic perspective to react negatively, by perhaps becoming envious and working less seriously in therapy. As mentioned, this can be very subtle. It may take the form of psychotherapists decorating their offices lavishly, being selfish and inflexible with their session or telephone consultation time, or talking down to the patient. What has traditionally been defended as professionalism may actually be a disguise for the expression of our most negative attributes concerning economic philosophy. These economic philosophies are not hidden. They are part of the factual economic reality that is apparent from the very beginning of the therapeutic relationship. Whether we come from a capitalistic or a collectivist perspective, no matter which side of the economic fence we sit on, we all—patients and psychotherapists alike—have both positive and negative attributes that express themselves at different times. The goal, like many of the issues that present themselves in the factual dimension, is not to try and undo the effects of the philosophies, but rather to acknowledge the differences and to neutralize the damaging systemic effects that may result from patient and psychotherapist interchange. If we move this issue to a level of awareness, we will have a better chance of not letting the factual determinant derail or confuse the therapy.

CHAPTER 3

It's Not Just Anxiety

The role of emotion in human experience is clearly an important factor in individual psychology, and no psychological theory simultaneously accounts for the mental events for more than one person. Yet the events that occur in the environment are taken in by an individual through sensing, perceiving, acting, and relating to the psyches of others, and these events shape and mold that individual's personality and psychology (Boszormenyi-Nagy & Krasner, 1986). Although the contextual perspective has traditionally used the theoretical positions of a number of orientations, including those of Adler, Freud, Jung, Rogers, and Gestalt (Boszormenyi-Nagy & Krasner, 1986), we would like to postulate a simplified perspective of individual psychology for the purpose of maximizing the understanding used in assessment, diagnosis, and interventions.

The fundamental belief of all individual psychological theories is that people are either created or influenced in such a way as to be affected by the environment and the relations around them. As individuals either strive or react to the world around them, they construct beliefs about who they are as individuals and how they should react to the world around them. This makes an individual's psychology subjective in nature, in that people who experience similar situations and backgrounds may develop very different ideas concerning themselves and their interactions. No matter what these constructions are, however, they serve as the basis from which the individual begins to be motivated by either aggression or ambivalence to strive for recognition, love, power, pleasure, or mastery (Boszormenyi-Nagy & Krasner, 1986).

The construction of individual psychology takes place in a subjective manner, but there is a consistent methodology to the construction. The elements that play an essential role reside in the structure of the brain, which sets the stage for human beings emotional reaction to the environment. In turn, this emotional reaction may become a predictable, or at least a well-used, pattern. As individuals proceed through development to cognitive thought, they construct ideas and beliefs about their personalities that will further shape ideas about themselves and their interactions with the environment. In this chapter, we will explore this model of how the psychology of individuals develops.

OBSERVATIONS CONCERNING ESSENTIAL CONSTRUCTS

Love and trust form essential constructs from which an understanding of emotions and personality can be drawn. At birth, children are particularly vulnerable and, in many ways, totally dependent upon the environment to take care of them. Because the cognitive structures of the child are extraordinarily tentative and undeveloped, leaving the child to depend primarily on lower brain functions (Rice, 2000), this early stage of development has a dramatic effect on the future relating of the child. The early attachment of the child to a significant caretaker is often considered a critical aspect of the child establishing an emotional link (Ainsworth & Bowlby, 1991) and desiring to maintain human contact through touching, listening, talking, or looking (Pipp & Harmon, 1987). This type of attachment is thought to be crucial to the child developing a sense of self and a desire for eventual socialization (Pipp, Easterbrooks, & Harmon, 1992). These contacts are essential, in that they serve as the basis for interactions that eventually shape personality. In contrast, children who are unattached or insecurely attached may display rejecting behavior of human attention or be emotionally insecure when left by themselves (Lieberman, Weston, & Pawl, 1991). All of this bonding and attachment largely takes place before verbalization in the cerebral cortex is functioning.

It is not only the developing sense of self that is important to these infants; children must also learn that the environment is trustworthy and secure. For instance, if children do not receive regular and adequate feedings, they are prone to develop anxiety (Valenzuela, 1990). Emotional cuddling and physical contact are essential for improvement in physical, cognitive, and social growth and are shown to be especially important for high-risk infants (Pelaez-Noguera, Gerwirtz, Field, Cigales, Malthurs, Clasky, & Sanchez, 1996). Emotional tension in the environment has been shown to have direct negative impact on children (Davies & Cummings, 1998).

At crucial points of child development, individuals construct meaning around two realities: (1) beliefs about self; and (2) beliefs about how to act or behave in relationships (Hargrave & Metcalf, 2000). In the context of how they are loved by caretakers and how trustworthy their primary relationships are, they consistently construct ideas about who they are and how they should act in relationships. This construction of reality around central concepts is similar to the way that Chomsky (1972) explains the nativist theory of language acquisition (Hargrave & Metcalf, 2000). Chomsky believes that individuals have a Language Acquisition Device, or LAD, that allows humans to access and make language in consistent ways. As children are exposed to language during the course of normal development, they will access and learn the language in a consistent way around constructs that will allow for objects and actions, as well as for syntax and grammar. Although children will speak different languages, depending on which one they are exposed to, all children go about learning language in the LAD in the same sequence, with similar development and characteristics.

In many ways, this is consistent with the postmodern constructivist view that there are multiple socially constructed realities, as speaking and the usage of multiple global languages suggest (Goldenberg & Goldenberg, 2000). However, Chomsky's theory does posit that there is a consistent methodology *in the manner or method* by which language is constructed. Similarly, humans have this consistent construct or device that requires them to make meaning around who they are and how they should act in a relationship. Humans will come to very different constructions about who they are and how they behave, but just as all languages have words for objects and actions, so do humans have constructions of beliefs about the self and how to behave in the world. Hargrave and Metcalf (2000) explain that humans come into the world with two spools that have no thread. As they experience love and trust or the lack of these two constructs—especially in childhood but also as adults—they formulate self-concepts for dealing with love and approaching future relationships with trust. From the contextual therapy perspective, as individuals experience the objectifiable and external dimensions of facts and systemic interactions, they make meaning in the subjective and internal dimensions of individual psychology and relational ethics.

Importance and Effect of Love

Although it is difficult to define love, there are various ways to conceptualize how love helps to form individual psychology. One way is to conceptualize love in the context of feelings that include connect-edness, warmth, passion, and sexual excitement (Grunebaum, 1997). We can describe this kind of love as erotic or romantic because it is characterized by a strong desire to be physically and emotionally intimate, idealization, and preoccupation (Hargrave, 2000).

Still another way to conceptualize love is in the context of inter-actions (Hargrave, 2000). These interactions are activities within a relationship that meet the needs of companionship, trust, and toler-ance. Here, love encompasses the essential elements of friendship and includes enjoyment, assistance, respect, acceptance, understand-ing, and admiration. We can describe this conceptualization as com-panionate love (Saxton, 1993). Finally, we can conceptualize love within the context of giving or sacrifice. Here, love means people giving up what they need or want for the good of the loved one (Hargrave, 2000). This love can be conceptualized as altruistic love (Saxton, 1993).

When we speak about individuals forming their self-concepts around the way they were initially loved, all three types of love are involved. Although varying degrees of each type of love are needed in different developmental periods, each type of love communicates something essential about our beings as individuals (Hargrave, 2000). Although we may think that erotic/romantic love is reserved only for sexual or mating relationships, it serves an essential role in our formation of self because family members love in this manner. When a young child is adored, holds the fascination of parents because of his or her habits and actions, and is the subject of focus and attention, the child cannot help but feel special. As children see themselves through the eyes of these loving family members, they see flawless, unique, and precious individuals. Erotic/romantic love assures us that nobody is quite like us and that we are highly prized (Hargrave, 2000).

Companionate love is usually associated with friendships, and rightly so. When we receive this type of love, we know that when we face the hard issues of life, someone will be there to give us support and assistance. This type of love, however, is also necessary from our families as we grow. So many things in life are out of our control. Accidents, threats to physical health, natural disaster, and financial ruin are just a few of the threats that can impinge on our safety. We cannot stop most of these uncontrollable problems from happening, but we can depend on the fact that our deepest relationships will give us support and companionship during the problems. This type of love, therefore, is an essential element for young children as they come to realize that no matter what happens in life, they will not be alone (Hargrave, 2000).

Altruistic love is perhaps the most misunderstood type of love. In our humanistic age, we have come to believe that altruism is the same as *unconditional positive regard* (Rogers, 1961). Unconditional positive regard primarily relates to accepting individuals just as they are, without having expectations that they will change. Altruism, however, carries the high price of sacrifice. For instance, if two people are on the brink of starvation and there is enough food for only one, the person who gives up his or her request for or right to the food is loving altruistically. The person who encourages the other to take the food is giving up something that is absolutely essential for his or her survival. The giving is not out of charity but out of sacrifice and altruism. This altruistic type of love communicates to the recipient that he or she is worthy. If people love us in this manner, it means that they count us as so important that they are willing to sacrifice what is wanted or needed for their own well-being. Although many family members and others are no doubt willing to sacrifice their lives so that their loved ones might live, this type of altruistic love can also be communicated in the mundane aspects of life. One example is when parents put their needs for food or clothing after those of their children. In little physical and emotional ways, when individuals sacrifice their wants and needs so that we may have ours fulfilled, we form the knowledge that we are people of great worth (Hargrave, 2000).

If we think of these three types of love working together, it is evident what is needed for an individual to form a healthy self-concept. Through erotic/romanic love, we learn that we are *unique* and *precious.* Companionate love teaches us *that we are not alone.* Finally, altruistic love teaches us that we are *worthy* as individuals. On the other hand, any time there is an absence of any or all of these particular types of love, young children are left to construct their ideas about self, wondering whether they are unique, precious, alone, or worthy. The absence of love teaches us that something is essentially flawed within ourselves that made us unacceptable to love.

Importance and Effect of Trust

Love is essential in the formation of the individual self-concept but is not the whole story. Especially in Western societies, we have had a tendency to perpetuate the belief that love can cure all problems and is the only thing necessary to have secure relationships. Trust is just as essential for healthy development and sound relationships because it is the primary relational resource from which we learn how to interact with others (Hargrave, 2000). The contribution of understanding trustworthiness as an essential relational resource is perhaps the most important attribute of contextual family therapy.

In contextual family therapy, trustworthiness is built upon the idea that we have an innate sense of justice that demands that we try to balance what we are entitled to receive from a relationship and what we are obligated to give in order to maintain it. In simple terms, in every relationship we are entitled to take something for ourselves and are obligated to give something back to the other person. The give-and-take in a relationship should be balanced or just, so that we feel that the relationship is fair.

In order to demonstrate how trustworthiness works in relationships, let us think of a simple symmetrical relationship like the ones that exist between spouses. Because relationships rely on a balance of this obligation (give) and merit (take), we can illustrate them by a bookkeeping account in a ledger. In table 3.1, a relational ledger is illustrated for a husband and wife. The left side of the ledger accounts for the merit (take) that a spouse would be entitled to receive from his or her partner: respect, care, and spousal intimacy. On the right side of the ledger is listed what the spouse's obligations (give) would be to his or her partner. The same give-and-take is listed because that is what is required to maintain a balanced, symmetrical, or fair relationship between the spouses (Hargrave, 2000).

When this type of balance occurs between giving what the relationship requires and receiving that to which individuals are entitled, then the spouses feel that the relationship is fair. If the balance continues over a longer period of time, then the spouses experience *trust* in one another. This trustworthiness, in turn, allows the spouses to engage in free giving of their obligations, without worry or concern that their own merit will be received. They are free to give because they *trust* that the other will give to them what they need (Hargrave, 2000).

The balance of the give-and-take in these types of relationships does not need to be exact at any given moment. Indeed, as spouses

TABLE 3.1
Illustration of Spousal Ledger

Merit or Take (What Individuals Are Entitled To)	Obligations or Give (What Individuals Are Obligated to Give)
1. Respect 2. Care 3. Intimacy	1. Respect 2. Care 3. Intimacy

interact in relationships, at times one gives more to the relationship than one receives, and at other times one receives more than one gives. It is the balance of the relationship over a period of time that makes for trustworthiness (Hargrave & Anderson, 1992). It is like a tightrope walker making his way across a cable. He shifts his balance back and forth many times in order to keep the overall balance. So it is with relationships. There is an oscillation between give and take as we move through life that allows us to maintain overall balance and to build trustworthiness in relationships.

On the other hand, when this balance breaks down, there are severe relational consequences. If one spouse feels that he or she gives all the time but never receives anything from the relationship, that person will soon feel the frustration of being cheated out of the just entitlement deserved. Instead of feeling free to give because he or she trusts the spouse to give in return, distrust will result. When distrust infiltrates a relationship, relational partners then move to threats and manipulation in efforts to get what they deserve. The results of these threats and manipulations are almost always damaging to the relationship and can easily result in the termination of the relationship. The spouses may love each other very much, but the lack of trust can easily destroy the relationship.

The previous example is an illustration of how trustworthiness functions in a spousal relationship. Spousal relationships, like those of friends and siblings, are called *horizontal relationships* because the relational demands between give and take are equal between partners (Boszormenyi-Nagy & Krasner, 1986). Trustworthiness is also, however, an essential resource in a relationship between successive generations, like that of parent and child. These types of relationships are called *vertical relationships* because the demand of give-and-take is not equal between the partners but is balanced throughout the generations. For instance, a parent is required to give love, security, and nurture to his or her child, whereas the child is not expected to give any such action in return. Although this is not balanced in the relationship between the parent and the child, it is balanced through the generations because parents were once children who received love, security, and nurture from their parents and children will be required to give love, security, and nurture to their children when they become parents (Hargrave & Anderson, 1992). Trustworthiness between generations has a dramatic effect on the dimension of relational ethics that will be discussed in chapter 5, but it is essential here to understand how trustworthiness is a resource that enables relational partners to give to one another and to interact in a healthy manner.

As children mature, they are exposed to either balanced trust-worthy relationships or untrustworthy relationships. If children see the horizontal relationships around them with people interacting in a balanced way and they experience appropriate giving and expecta-tions in their relationship with their parents, then children are likely to learn that relationships are safe places to interact and that they can trust others and give freely. If, however, children see threats and manipulation in the horizontal relationships around them and have unfair expectations put on them by their parents, they will learn that relationships are dangerous and will construct the idea that one must find a way to protect oneself from other people. Two primary ele-ments are essential in building a stable give-and-take relationship so that individuals know how to act in future relationships. These are responsibility and reliability (Hargrave, 2000).

Responsibility. The basic idea behind responsibility is that people know and acknowledge the actions and behaviors of giving that rightly belong to them. This is especially important with regard to young children. When children are very young, there is little they can do in the way of self-care. The parents are responsible for making sure that children are emotionally and physically cared for in an adequate fash-ion. If parents, however, shirk the responsibility and take care of their own needs first, then children will no doubt grow up learning that they will have to take care of themselves. This scenario is, of course, sad and unfortunate because these children will likely grow up with the perspective that all relationships are secondary to the care of oneself. But even more damaging is when parents do not take appro-priate responsibility for children but instead require young children to take parental responsibility in making the parents feel emotionally and physically cared for. The children will try to fulfill this responsi-bility but will fail miserably because of lack of maturity and because it is not fairly their responsibility. This scenario usually sets the stage for even more unfortunate actions, as the parents become frustrated with the children. But more damaging is the fact that the children will likely grow to feel justified in not taking their appropriate responsi-bilities in relationships and will look for other innocent parties to exploit and to take their obligations.

Responsibility essentially means that we take the obligations to give that rightly belong to us and we actually give. It also means that we do not steal the entitlements of others in our relationships or take the merits that rightly belong to them. Responsibility is about rela-tional partners fulfilling their roles and doing what those relational roles dictate.

Reliability. Taking responsibility for doing what one is supposed to do in a relationship is not enough to build trustworthiness. It is also essential that people carry out their responsibilities in a consistent manner (Hargrave, 2000). Picture, if you will, alcoholics who continue to drink. They may acknowledge their responsibility in any particular relationship but may not carry out the responsibility in any disciplined or consistent fashion because they are impaired by the drug. When giving is not reliable, trustworthiness is impossible (Hargrave, 2000).

Reliability, however, does not mean perfection. There will be times in even the best of relationships when relational partners are unreliable. But in order for trustworthiness to be built in relationships, people do need to perform their responsibilities 90 to 95% of the time. Unless we have this type of overwhelming evidence that relationships are reliable, we are forced into the position of questioning and distrust.

Trustworthiness is therefore just as essential a resource as love is when it comes to forming individual psychology. When children are exposed to trustworthy relationships through observation and experience responsible and reliable giving from caretakers, they will likely learn how to interact with others in this same responsible, reliable, and trustworthy manner. If children observe and experience unstable and untrustworthy relationships, they will at best believe that self-reliance and protection are essential in relationships and, at worst, will believe that they are justified in being irresponsible, unreliable, and untrustworthy in order to get what they need physically or emotionally.

OBSERVATIONS CONCERNING BRAIN STRUCTURE AND EMOTION

So, if love and trust are essential constructs in the formation of a healthy individual psychology, what occurs when individuals do not come from these loving and trustworthy environments? Midbrain activity is much more influential in a child's early formations (Hockenbury & Hockenbury, 2000). Part of the limbic system, the amygdala, is heavily involved in controlling a variety of innate human emotions, including fear and anger (Aggleton, 1992). The two emotions of fear and anger, when felt, are essential in triggering the fight-or-flight response, which physically prepares us to use our power to fight or our anxiety to flee (Cannon, 1932). It is also clear from the research that the amygdala is heavily involved in learning and in forming memories that possess a strong emotional component (LeDoux, 1994). Research suggests that any outside stimulus that humans are exposed to activates the amygdala, which in turn produces the emotional responses of fear or anger (LeDoux, 1996). These responses and subsequent reactions are formed *separately from cognitive processing* (LeDoux, 1996).

If individuals, in their early formation, are exposed to loving caretakers who respond in a consistent and trustworthy way, the amygdala is not stimulated by stress and people have no need to react to the stress with fear or anger. On the contrary, this love and trust in the environment are likely to stimulate pleasurable and rewarding sensations (Olds, 1958). When, however, the individual is exposed to unloving or untrustworthy caregivers, the environment stresses the person and the amygdala responds to the stress with the primary emotions of either fear or anger. The individual, at a very primitive and basic level, responds to the threat to self (love) and environment (trust).

Although these emotional responses and actions are formed separately from the cognitive processes, cognition does perceive and process the responses and reactions after they have occurred (LeDoux, 1996). In other words, once there has been a stress and the reaction of fear or anger, cognition makes sense of the experience. We believe that individuals cognitively transform the pain and stress from their lack of care and nurture into feelings about the self (primarily, violations of love) and beliefs about actions they must take in future relationships (primarily, violations of trust). As figure 3.1 illustrates, when people are violated, they are likely to feel (1) resulting rage, as they experience uncontrolled anger toward those who should have provided love; or (2) shame as they accuse themselves of being unlovable and not deserving of a nurturing relationship. Similarly, people are likely to take actions in future relationships that are (1) overcontrolling, as they try to minimize their risk of being hurt in relationships; or (2) chaotic, as they assume that little can be done to form trusting relationships and that they will eventually be hurt despite any effort (Hargrave, 2001).

These emotions are seen in the extreme as the severity of violations of love and trust in relationships increases (Hargrave, 2001). *Rage* consists of an internal feeling of anger and external actions that are in response to the belief that the primary caretakers were irresponsible in expressing love. The individual feels wronged about the lack of love received and therefore feels justified in retaliatory rage in response. *Shame,* on the other hand, is seen as an internal feeling of

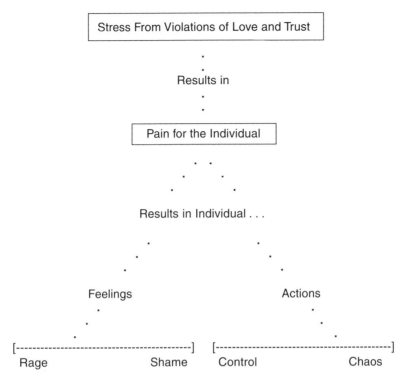

FIGURE 3.1. Model of Violations of Love and Trust

guilt or unworthiness in response to the caretakers' lack of love. In-stead of blaming the caretaker, individuals who feel shame internalize the lack of nurture as a feeling that they are unlovable. *Control* is a methodology of action in which individuals seek involvement that does not leave them open to exploitation in relationships. As these types of individuals experience relationships as untrustworthy, they determine that they will protect themselves by managing all aspects of life and risking little in relationships. *Chaos,* however, is the oppo-site methodology in response to a violation of trust. In this response, individuals assume that life is unmanageable and there is little that they can do to make situations reliable or trustworthy. As a result, these types of individuals usually avoid organization and responsibil-ity and take advantage of situations that will add stimulation to their lives, such as overspending or abusing drugs and alcohol. It is impor-tant to realize that individuals who experience love and trust viola-tions may experience any or all of these emotional responses in any combination (Hargrave, 2001). For instance, consider the following dialogue from a therapy session, in which the patient is a young woman who was severely physically abused by her mother and her father.

Woman: There was one time that I remember my mother yelling at me and she grabbed a bottle and clubbed me with it. I was 11 years old.

Therapist: (Long pause) That is awful.

Woman: I went into my room. Later, when my father came to get me, he saw the blood on my bed. You know what he did? He yelled and cursed me for being so stupid to get blood on the bed. (Long pause) It seems I have been wondering all my life about what is so wrong with me that my parents hated me so.

It is clear here that the woman internalized the violations of love and trust into a feeling of shame. Instead of blaming the people who abused her, she felt that something was wrong with her. In another example of abuse, a husband talks about his family of origin in marital therapy.

Husband: You say I'm always angry and controlling. Well, I have a lot to be angry about.

Wife: Why are you so angry with me?

Husband: I've been angry all my life. You didn't have to live with those idiots who are my parents. They beat the living daylights out of me and then they would say that they love me later. Assholes. (Long pause and then looks at the therapist.) I knew that when I finally got out of there, I would never let anyone take advantage of me again.

Therapist: Is that why you keep your wife to such tight and demanding rules?

Husband: I'm not ever going to be abused in any way ever again.

This man dealt with the violations of love and trust from his parents in a very different way from the previous woman. Instead of internalizing the violations into feelings of shame concerning himself, he was driven by feelings of rage toward his parents. In addition, he internalized his dealing with relationships into a very controlling perspective that assures him that he will be safe. In still another case of abuse, a man discussed his behavior with the therapist.

Man: You just don't realize how discouraging it is to wake up every day and face all the realities of the opportunities that got away. I could have been an airline pilot. I could have been an engineer. Everyone blames me for losing those opportunities, but it isn't true.

Therapist: What is the truth?

Man: The truth is that the airline never had any intention of making me a pilot. They were constantly on me about doing better in the training and leaving hints that I wasn't trying hard enough. One day—just one day—I snapped and said the hell with it.

Therapist: What happened?

Man: What happened is I got plastered. When I didn't show up, they terminated my training. (Long pause) They were stressing me out and they knew that I would break. I just accommodated them.

In this situation, the man came from a home where his father physically abused him and his mother. Although he was extraordinarily intelligent, he kept destroying his life by engaging in alcoholism and irresponsibility. He had internalized the violations of love and trust into some feelings of rage but predominately into actions involving chaos. He believed that the world was out to get him, so he sought chaotic escape by numbing himself with alcohol. Although all three of these cases illustrate individuals who experienced childhood abuse, they internalized the actions into very different manifestations of feelings and actions.

It is also necessary to point out that the extremes of rage and control are primarily power responses to threats that are likely stimulated by the basic emotion of anger in the amygdala and that give rise to a fight response. In addition, the extremes of shame and chaos are primarily anxiety responses to threats that are connected with the basic emotion of fear in the amygdala, which gives rise to a flight response. Much of the field of psychological study in the first 120 years of its existence has been built around the understanding of how anxiety complicates human emotions and behaviors. What we propose here is that anxiety responses are only half the story of the individual formation of personality and emotion. An equal player in the formation of individual psychology consists of the power responses.

When an individual in his or her early formation experiences either lack of love, lack of trust, or both, it is sufficient to prompt a

So what are meds trying to do about amygdala?

stressful perception in the amygdala, which in turn prompts the response of power reactions (fight) or anxiety reactions (flight). As these violations continue during early development and as anger and anxiety persist, cognitive perceptions begin the formation of the sense of self and the sense of actions in the environment (LeDoux, 1994). It is in this cognitive perception and the formation of the individual's psychology that the construction of emotions and behaviors are governed by a preference toward power responses (fight) or anxiety responses (flight) or both. The field of psychology has demonstrated a proficiency for dealing with anxiety responses; however, the attention that has been given to power responses is insufficient. Too often, psychotherapists' responses to these power issues of rage or control are to refer patients elsewhere, to ignore the responses, and, in some cases, to regard them as threats, in which law enforcement authorities should be involved. There is little doubt that individuals who have developed preferences toward power responses can be difficult and even dangerous, but these responses come from the same sources of violations as do anxiety responses. Exploration of the power responses in individual psychology with the same intensity that has been given to the anxiety responses is warranted.

Contextual therapy offers a methodology for understanding how love and trust form and shape the individual psychologies and emotions of people. If initial formative relationships were loving and trustworthy, then individual formation in the psychological sense of self and relational beliefs would be healthy and stable. If, however, these initial formative relationships produced violations of love and trust, the basic emotions of fear, anger, or both would be stimulated, causing the individual experiencing the violation to build emotional feelings in the direction of rage, shame, or both and emotional reactions to relationships that expressed control or chaos.

CONTEXTUAL THERAPY
AND INDIVIDUAL PSYCHOLOGY

If we can better understand the nature of the dimension of individual psychology, what difference does it make in psychotherapy? This type of contextual understanding can have far-reaching effects into how we proceed with psychotherapy in this dimension, particularly in the areas of assessment/diagnosis, treatment focus, interventions in current relationships, and teaching self-care for the patient.

Assessment/Diagnosis

It is an unfortunate reality that much of what is done in the psychiatric and psychological fields is driven by symptomolgy. Our assessments of individuals, diagnostic codes, and treatment goals are often driven by the patient's symptomology. Diagnosis is important for communication within the scientific community but offers only a few tools for treatment. However, the previously proposed understanding of the individual psychology dimension offers the psychotherapist an opportunity to view human beings outside of their symptomology. First, it deals with the most basic elements that form human feelings and behaviors. Although we do not propose that the previous model is sufficient for understanding the total complexity of human beings, it offers a rudimentary understanding of the most basic elements with which humans construct ideas about themselves and actions toward the environment. It gives, therefore, the psychotherapist the ability to focus on the *causes* of behaviors and to view symptomology only in terms of *responses* to violations of love and trust. For instance, the following is a case excerpt of a woman who is in controlling/chaotic and shame/raging cycles.

Woman: I guess that what they say about me is true. I am a borderline.

Therapist: Why do you believe that it's true?

Woman: It must be true. One minute I feel like I can do anything and that I don't need anybody; the next I'm so frightened to be alone that I would give anything to have someone just hold me. Then when I find someone, I feel like they are somehow out to get me or they lie to me. I just feel so frightened and at the same time so angry. (Starts to cry.) That's when I get so confused and desperate.

Therapist: What happens when you become confused and desperate?

Woman: I just have to leave. I run away. Sometimes I get so upset that I just think about ramming my car into a concrete wall.

Therapist: And you think that the reason that you have all these strange, erratic emotions is that you have a borderline personality?

Woman: Well, isn't it?

Therapist: I don't think so. I think that in your very early formation about who you are and how you should act, the world must have seemed like a dangerous and rejecting place. You might have been forced to do things that you should have never had to do, you might have been abused or taken advantage of, you might have been left to take care of yourself—I don't know the specifics, but I believe that things were probably not what you or I would call a loving and trustworthy environment.

Woman: (Long pause) Well, I think that maybe all those things are true.

Therapist: Then I would not see what you feel or how you act as a result of some personality disorder; I believe that you have learned to think about yourself and act in certain ways as an effort to cope with the craziness that surrounded you at certain points of your life. Those beliefs and reactions are still happening because you may still feel that life is not safe and that maybe you are still not okay.

Woman: (Long pause) Well, is there hope for me to get out?

Therapist: I believe so, but we will have to understand those violations and then work on different ways of confronting those issues than the ones that come out of your feelings and beliefs.

Here the therapist did not accept a diagnosis based on symptomology. She instead focused her attention on the cause of the symptomology. This not only promoted a sense of hopefulness for the patient, it gave the patient an opportunity to define her actions in the context of coping or defenses. This process then gave the psychotherapist the opportunity to work on the causes of behavior in order to address the symptomology, instead of the other way around.

Treatment Focus

Often, psychotherapists get trapped into simply working only on behavior. There are appropriate times for behavioral treatment; however, when behaviors stem from individual psychology issues, it is more appropriate to focus on the original violations. For instance, many times when patients experience enormous rage reactions, behaviorally we may try to get them to focus on something relaxing or calming. When someone is exhibiting chaotic behavior, we typically may focus the therapy on building more structure or on organizing elements into the patients' lives. The fact is that oftentimes we as psychotherapists try to move people along the continuums of feelings and behaviors found in figure 3.1. We try to get blaming, raging people to focus on themselves, whereas we try to get shaming people to move the focus and blame off themselves and onto others. We try to make controlling people more chaotic and chaotic people more controlling. Of course, these kinds of behavioral shifts are futile. If, indeed, people respond emotionally and actively in these ways because of violations in the type of love and trustworthiness that they experienced, only focusing treatment on those violations holds a hope of eventually changing beliefs, feelings, and behaviors.

Interventions in Current Relationships

Many times people react to others in a way that is reminiscent of their old relationships. This is sometimes because the pattern of behavior and emotion is set, but often it is a result of the current relationship stimulating some reminder of the past. For instance, the following is from a case where a man experienced tremendous rage when his wife made what she believed to be a harmless gesture.

Husband: I saw our son throw some tissue out of the car window and I just blew up. She just sat there with this look on her face like I was a madman.

Wife: (Smiles slightly.) It was a tissue.

Husband: (Very angry) This is exactly what she did! I try and teach the kids the right behavior and she is always taking their side and won't support me in the least! (Yelling) I don't have to put up with this kind of treatment!

Therapist: I want you to be supported. Tell me, do you remember other times that you were not supported and were left on your own besides with your wife?

Husband: It used to happen to me all the time when I was a kid. I was told to pick up things around the house or take out the garbage. I would do it and never would get a word of appreciation. Then when something was broken or not done around the house, I always got the blame. I was never respected in the least, even though I worked the hardest.

Therapist: It seems to me that this situation with your wife not sup-
porting you and laughing at you when your son threw the
tissue out the window felt just like another time you were
not respected or appreciated.

Husband: Just one more time. She does it all the time.

Therapist: I do want to address this with your wife, but I am wondering if all the times you were not respected or appreciated
by the family you grew up in are like bullets that hit you a
long time ago that weren't removed. The skin healed over
so the wounds look healed, but every time the places
where the bullet entered get hit, it hurts just like you were
being shot all over again. In other words, maybe your
wife is just hitting an old injury.

Husband: That's probably true, but it still hurts my feelings.

Therapist: Indeed, but maybe if you and I can understand the old
wounds, we can separate them out so that they don't get
hit by people who really aren't trying to hurt you at all.

Instead of tailoring the intervention to involve the husband and
wife interaction, the therapist first sought an intervention to deal with
the heart of what made the husband upset. This type of intervention
not only held the potential of helping the husband realize that he
would need to separate his reactions to his past relationships from
current ones, it also gave his wife an understanding of what behaviors or actions on her part would stimulate special sensitivity and hurt
in the husband. Simply put, our understanding of individual psychology allows us to get the right actors with the right script.

Teaching Self-Care for the Patient

When people experience violations of love and trust in their families
of origin, it is difficult to make these right. Unfortunately, psychotherapists hold little power to modify an individual's psychology. It is
not because we do not mean well or even that we do not have an
important role to play in healing; it is because we do not hold family
membership with our patients. Only one source is powerful enough
to teach individuals that they are loved and that the world is trustworthy. It is the patient's family of origin. By the time we see our patients
in therapy, they have the essential and most important constructions
already made concerning their personhoods and how to react in relationships.

For some patients, there are some opportunities to rework love and trust in their families. For many, however, either the families are no longer available or the interactions would simply offer more evidence of how our patients are not loved and their families are not trustworthy. Especially in these cases, our work in individual psychology is most important. In creating a situation of insight into how the formation of self and of actions in relationships took place in our patients, we give them the opportunity to grow past such misinformation. Although we as psychotherapists may not be powerful enough to rewrite our patients' histories of love and trust, in many cases they themselves may be able to become that powerful.

In teaching our patients about self-care, we first must give them insight regarding the formation of their personalities. In encouraging their maturity, we extend the invitation to them about making a choice between being the person who was formed in their past or being who they can become. In making this type of choice, patients do so with the understanding that they must counter tendencies and beliefs that come naturally. They must learn to not always trust initial emotions and to actively question their beliefs about the relational reality. Most important, however, they must learn the essential elements that help them restructure and nurture themselves. Some of these essential elements may involve resources such as intentional relational substitutes, accessing and believing in spiritual resources, involvement in groups that are seeking the same restructuring, and even reading about the experiences of others. Some of these specific applications are discussed in chapter 6, but the primary idea here is that a contextual understanding of individual psychology provides the structure and insight necessary for individuals to begin the long but fruitful task of caring for themselves and at least countering the damaging effects of when love and trust violations taught them negative lessons about self and relationships.

CHAPTER 4

It's How You Play the Game

Contextual family therapy has been a part of the family therapy movement from the very beginning, as Boszormenyi-Nagy was a key figure in applying systems thinking to families (Goldenberg & Goldenberg, 2000). Relational ethics, however, have been such an essential part of the contextual approach that many therapists tend to neglect the interventions that are possible in this third dimension. Systemic interventions offer the contextual therapist a wide variety of treatment opportunities and integrations with other family theories, as long as those interventions do not violate the ethical mandates of the intergenerational family. As such, this chapter gives an overview of the systemic theoretical background and several techniques that we have found useful with families. Although many of these interventions belong to other family therapy approaches, the third dimension allows the contextual therapist to integrate some of these useful techniques into effective treatment interventions.

The dimension of systemic interactions is all about the medium of communication in any type of relationship. Stated another way, it is the method by which the system lets members know how they are regarded and what rules and beliefs govern their interactions. Because this dimension is systemic, it concerns any type of interactions, whether or not these have anything to do with families. For instance, the same interactions and belief patterns that govern a family may be found in a corporate business structure or a government. It is in the family, however, where we learn the most important rules of systemic interaction. The family is the setting where most of us interacted first and developed our knowledge of how life and relationships worked. Families are not limited to just a traditional conceptualization but also include life partnerships among cohabiting people or any group formation in which people take responsibility for one another, have the responsibility of raising children, or both. Because the family is so important in the formation of individuals and in governing any change that is possible, we will concentrate here on the systemic interactions that exist in the family.

The dimension of systemic interactions, as stated earlier, really relies on the framework of general systems theory. The dimension is objectifiable because most of the interactive components can readily be observed. Of primary importance in this dimension, however, is its power to produce change in the nature of relationships and to show how to use this knowledge to produce change. Most of these interactions can directly be observed; others are invisible, but their consequences are visible.

WHY ARE FAMILIES SO IMPORTANT?

Politicians and churches once emphasized the importance of family, usually by using arguments based on morals. As psychotherapists, we have to stress the importance of the family for individual growth, for relating, and for dealing with social reality. In the family, infants learn to express emotions, and while in contact with their parents, they learn to differentiate emotions. Children develop not only the basic impulses relating to their physical being but also the interactions that will teach conscience, values, and beliefs. As psychotherapists, we know the horrible effects on the individual's psychology if violations of love, trust, or both occur in the family. We can observe the effects of the family atmosphere on the development of the self, for example, regarding self-esteem and ego strength. But we also see how the interactions shape the social self of the child; the way he or she relates is heavily influenced by the style of the particular family. For instance, the experience of our families of origin will strongly influence our willingness and our capacities to satisfy the emotional needs of our partners (love) and to enter into fair giving and receiving (trustworthiness). Again, if a family sees the world as dangerous and intrusive, this will strongly influence the attitude of family members toward the outer world and social reality, and the family may develop into more of a fortress than a social interactive group.

A family must be seen as a complete system. It produces basic experiences of how to deal with emotions, intimacy, conflict, and social reality, which shape the individual psychology. Even highly individual psychological structures like self-esteem are the result of communication and interaction, including one's subjective way of interpreting these interactions. The best way to understand how a system like a family works is not by investigating the members' individual psychologies, but rather their systemic interactions.

CONCEPTUALIZING COMMUNICATION AND JOINING

Paul Watzlawick (1967) proposed a pragmatic theory of communication, which is still fundamental for systemic thinking. He puts forth the idea that communication can be reduced to seven basic premises.

1. It is impossible not to communicate. Even withdrawal or saying nothing will be noticed and interpreted by others as being shy or rude.
2. Whenever communication has two angles—one that is rational and the other emotional—the emotional communication is more powerful in shaping the relationship.
3. The kind of relationship between two persons is determined by the way they interpret sequences of communication.
4. Human communication uses digital, verbal, and analogue channels such as gestures, facial expressions, and signals. Usually, the nonverbal ways of communication are more important but less clear. People use other information, such as background information or the context of the communication, to get a clear idea about what is meant.
5. Repetitive ways of interaction can be called a rule or a pattern. Patterns are usually fixed by cycles of communication. Repetitive patterns build a structure, which usually is not conscious, but we can observe it. In systemic thinking the fundamental questions are "What are the rules?" "How does the system work?" and "What cycles of communication perpetuate the structure?"
6. A family or a couple does not see cycles of communication but usually thinks in very subjective patterns of cause and effect. For instance, a wife might grumble because her husband always drinks, whereas the husband might be angry and believe that he drinks because his wife always grumbles.
7. Patterns of communication can be symmetrical, meaning that both partners try to do the same things in a competitive way, or complementary, which is based on partners doing asymmetrical or different things, such as one partner being strong, while the other is weak. Symmetrical systems tend to be escalating, whereas complementary systems tend be very stable but hard to change.

These suppositions still serve us well in the therapeutic field, as we seek to understand the nature of this objectifiable dimension. We watch the interactions in order to determine the intricacies of how power, organization, and beliefs are formed within the family. But understanding patterns is not enough. As contextual therapists, we do not conceive of ourselves as neutral. We have a global or strategic orientation to move a person, a couple, or a family away from a situation of despair, suffering, having symptoms, or dysfunctional behavior. We want to help them to change toward suffering less and getting along better in life and in their relationships by using the powerful resources of love and trust. True therapy, from a contextual perspective, will try to induce processes of restructuring.

In order to achieve this restructuring, we recognize the importance of establishing a good working alliance with the family. All therapy outcome research reveals the importance of a good connection between the psychotherapist and patients. Contextual therapists do not take an expert position but rather believe in the concept that all members of the family system have claims and interests that are justified. All family members have performed actions that are constructive, whereas other actions are destructive. The therapist joins in a working alliance with the family by recognizing each member's claims, interests, and actions. Fair consideration of all family members not only joins the psychotherapist with the family but also sets a trustworthy framework for the possibilities of change.

After the psychotherapist joins with the family, the first tactical steps are to create an atmosphere of working together for constructive change. Achieving this atmosphere sometimes requires only 10 minutes, whereas in other situations we will need much more time. The first questions that psychotherapists must ask themselves revolve around the reason that the person or the family is coming to therapy. Is the context that the patients want therapy for themselves? Do they feel that the other family members are the problem? Are they forced to see the therapist by court order? Have they felt rejected by other psychotherapists or physicians? Are they coming to therapy because another family member is threatening to leave? Does a man see me because his wife threatens to leave him if he won't undergo therapy? All of these questions are important to analyze, at least to determine if the family members are open to the idea of change.

Most patients and families are burdened, often overwhelmed, by anxiety and feelings of guilt and shame. The next important task of the psychotherapist is to reduce these overwhelming burdens. This is partly done by relating, but more specific comments are usually necessary. Anxiety, depression, bad relationships, or a diagnosis of psychological problems can shatter one's self-concept and provoke deep shame. This can be utilized by the therapist as an opportunity to demonstrate the interactions of fair giving and receiving. For example, a psychotherapist may respond to patients in a variety of ways, in order to communicate this new respect and way of interacting.

- I assume that it is difficult to talk about personal problems to a man you hardly know, but I think you are doing it to help your family.
- This is a therapy session and we will not put blame on anyone. We will simply seek to take responsibility.
- Guilt always requires what lawyers call "animus auctoris," or the intent to cause harm. I do not know yet about you, but in my experience, most people do not intend to cause harm.
- I do not know about your family yet, but I have learned from my work with incest survivors that there could be severe guilt feelings without any real reason. The victimized child is not guilty and we have to shatter this belief in order to be successful.

In contextual therapy, we are always concerned with communicating to the individual or the family that we are interested in locating strengths and resources; promoting transformations that produce love, trust, and fair giving; and intervening to stop destructive actions.

FREQUENT PROBLEMS AND INTERACTION TRAPS

Medical and psychology students are trained over the years to find out what is wrong, "to chase pathology." Antonovsky (1984) was the first to ask the question the other way around: How do people manage to stay healthy despite medical, psychological, and social risk factors? It is certainly difficult to describe "the healthy family," but we can use Antonovsky's approach and ask, "What are families that stay healthy or normal doing differently from those families we see in therapy?" At least in general terms, these healthy functions can be described as a capacity to problem-solve, to change according to the family life cycle, to balance closeness and distance, to respect the boundaries between the generations, and to develop and maintain a common belief system. This list could be extended but is probably sufficient to help us understand how difficult and complex these tasks are for a family amid the requirements of earning money, providing housing, and giving security.

Several systems for family health have been suggested, but it is important to realize from a contextual perspective that many of them lack the orientation that accounts for an oscillation between the process of give-and-take or what Boszormenyi-Nagy and Krasner (1986) call "balance in motion." Some models are too complicated and are more of academic interest, but some of the factors are clinically important and can be helpful. Most models take into account factors like flexibility or capacity of adaptation. According to Reiss (1981), poor adaptation can be due to closure. For example, the family members feel threatened by new situations, and they tend to perceive only things they already know from the past. Poor adaptation can also be due to perceiving the outer world as frightening and chaotic. If we have bad adaptation to reality, this topic has to be addressed and it is important to find out whether it is due to lack of social skills, which can be improved by a specific training, or to conflict. In families, adaptation is an equivalent of reality testing in individuals, and mechanisms that deteriorate ego functions like reality testing have to be addressed.

Another important factor is cohesion. In every family we see, we have to ask ourselves whether centripetal forces, like those that may exist with anorectic or phobic members, or centrifugal forces, such as those that may exist in families with law-offending members, are predominant. Centripetal forces can be considered a type of bonding and can have different forms. Bonding by affect can reach as far as sexual abuse; cognitive bonding uses pressure on family members to share worldviews or an ideology. Another form of bonding uses feelings of loyalty to, for instance, prevent a family member from leaving the family and applying for a job in another city. In every relationship, the degree of emotional closeness and of distance has to be regulated. The desire that individuals perceive for more closeness or more distance is highly determined by family patterns of interaction. Families with too much closeness are usually described in terms of enmeshment (Minuchin, 1974) or intersubjective fusion (Boszormenyi-Nagy & Krasner, 1986), whereas families with too much distance are described as disengaged or isolated. Closeness is important for feeling loved, for developing the feeling of self, or in terms of Martin Buber's "das Ich wächst am Du" (I grow being in touch with Thou). On the other hand, distance is important for developing clear boundaries, being able to say no, or getting things done one's own way.

Healthy or functional families usually have a tolerance for ambivalence; dysfunctional families try to exclude ambivalence. One way is that the whole family moves toward one side, excluding the counterpart and ambivalence. Concerning the ambivalence of closeness and distance, excluding distance and centrifugal drives leads to enmeshment, as the whole family is rigidly stuck in closeness. Another possibility to exclude is collusion, or a rigid way of dividing roles within the family. When one family member always seeks closeness, the other one always wants distance. If one always has the power, the other one is always weak.

As with all complementary patterns, collusion is very stable, but it offers no chance for further growth. If the child of parents stuck in collusion produces symptoms like failure at school or bulimia, we can regard this as an attempt at problem solving. Both parents are forced to engage in closeness, giving, and caring, and at the same time they can maintain distance by accusing each other of having caused the child's problem. This example illustrates one of the contributions of systemic thinking and family therapy to the field of therapy: A symptom that seems to have no meaning or benefit for the individual can have a tremendous importance for the family and can make sense in this context.

A big problem, when there is collusion in a couple or a family, is that only one person seems to have an individual problem. In order to change a collusive pattern, the psychotherapist must: (1) ask the strong partner when he or she got help/emotional support from the partner and make the strong person acknowledge it, and (2) go back to the family of origin to find out why it was necessary not to show feelings. For example, the following is from a session with a couple that had been married for 10 years, and the wife was being treated for depression.

Therapist: We all see that Mary is depressed, which means it is very hard for her to be active or to perceive herself as a giving person. Bob, as you know her much better than I do, can you remember an example when she was an emotional support for you?

(Defining the problem of depression as a block of giving and receiving offers a therapeutic chance of removing that block.)

Husband: Well, I don't think I need much help.

Therapist: Sure, I have no doubt you can do your job on your own. But do you remember a situation, maybe years ago, when Mary was caring or supportive?

Husband: When my father got sick and then died 3 years ago, I had to work and travel a lot, and she went to my father's house regularly and helped care for him.

Therapist: Yes, this is a very good and helpful example of emotional
support. Mary is certainly depressed now, but your example shows her as a caring and giving person. How could
Mary notice that her caring for your father was helpful for
you?

Acknowledgment was appropriate, and the therapist asked how
it was expressed. If it was expressed, the therapist would acknowledge it and ask Mary whether she felt the acknowledgment. If it was
not expressed, this would offer a chance to talk about Bob's problems of emotional giving, which would lead most probably to his
family of origin.

Collusion is one specific way families try to keep relationships
free of ambivalence. This can be an obstacle in therapy or, to use
Freud's expression, can be interpreted as resistance. Table 4.1 shows
other reasons that families may be resistant in therapy.

TABLE 4.1
Reasons Family Members Are Resistant; Therapeutic Strategies

Resistance in Order to . . .	Beliefs	Therapeutic Strategies
Avoid ambivalence of closeness and distance.	—If I receive, I will be dependent. —I have to be thankful for things I don't want.	Fair giving and receiving in order to build trustworthiness.
Prevent change.	Separation is death.	1. Parents giving permission to leave. 2. Addressing family-of-origin issues.
Prevent conflict.	Conflict destroys love.	Different values and wishes can be tolerated and negotiated.
Maintain the power and position.	I am entitled to exploit others for what I need.	1. Address victimization in family of origin. 2. Address how the patient wants to be seen. 3. Time progression or postulating about the future.
Remain loyal.	Family mythology.	Do not challenge, but promote fair giving and receiving.

In families we may find power issues, emotional splitting, scapegoating, problem patterns like taking drugs or having affairs, parentification fusion, or disengagement. Beyond doubt, all these patterns can produce enormous suffering for family members and can block individual growth, as well as the growth of love and trust. But all these items can be addressed and utilized for a more profound understanding of ideas and experiences of the involved family members. As we see in dysfunctional families, resistance against the ambivalence of closeness and of distance usually rigidly excludes one possibility. Collusion is one way of avoiding closeness; another possibility is a pursuer/distancer pattern. This is usually accompanied either by fears of dependency (If I receive from others, I will be dependent) or by fears of manipulation. For example, the following is from a case where the wife was depressed after her husband had an operation to remove a cancer.

Husband: I don't want presents from my wife, not at my birthday, not when I'm at the hospital, and not at Christmas. She should learn to respect my privacy.

Therapist: Can you give an example of someone not respecting your privacy?

Husband: My mother used to stuff me with food and give me presents I didn't like. Then she would complain that I was not thankful.

Therapist: You felt manipulated by having to accept things you didn't want.

Husband: Exactly.

After that, a successful therapy started, the wife learned not to behave like her husband's mother, and the husband gave her chances for giving.

In cases of resistance in order to prevent change we often find ideas such as "Growing leads to separation" and "Separation is death." We frequently find histories of early losses, and family-of-origin work has to be done. This often makes it possible for parents to take responsibility for the further growth of their children and gives children permission to leave, instead of parents' demanding sacrifices from their children. Resistance in order to prevent conflict is also an attempt to avoid ambivalence. We often find families stuck in closeness and frequently displaying symptoms of phobia or anxiety. We usually find ideas and belief systems like "Conflict destroys love."

Some structures based on power are easy to detect; others are disguised. Boszormenyi-Nagy and Spark (1984) pointed out that the martyr in a family who prevents the other family members from acting out and getting rid of guilt feelings can have more power than the yelling tyrant. As described in chapter 3, power can best be understood as a method of defense and not as an individual trait. It makes a big difference whether I strive for power and whether it is practiced in an open or a hidden way. The husband who doesn't let his wife know details about his income or his bank account uses power but may disguise it as solicitude (i.e., I do not want to bother her with trivial things). When we start a family therapy session and ask, "What is the problem?" usually the one who answers has the power position. But in families that use power in a more disguised way, the power person will usually give nonverbal permission to another family member to express the problem. Power is important for individual growth, but it can be used in very destructive ways as well. Systems theory in the 1950s showed how power and the use of double binds in some families of schizophrenics can produce enormous psychological damage and can prevent the vulnerable person from self-delineation and self-object differentiation. We can observe subsystems or coalitions to maintain the power position, and these observations are significant. But it is even more important to find out the underlying ideas of the power person, as this will lead directly to the experienced violation of love and trust and to destructive actions. For example, a successful manager made his wife sign a marriage contract that financially made her completely dependent on him. In his own childhood he experienced never-ending conflicts between his parents; his alcoholic father often beat him up, whereas his much younger sister was his father's favorite. He had no guilt feelings for treating his wife unfairly, a clear indicator of his destructive actions. His preconscious ideas were that even a partner might treat him unfairly and that he had a right to exploit others.

Therapy, in order to be helpful in the previous situation, had to follow several guidelines when power issues were concerned. Before confronting this manager with his destructive behavior, I had to address his own victimization in his family of origin. A further step can be what Hargrave (2001) calls "insight." Insight means detecting and blocking the ways that destructive behavior is perpetuated. Changing the destructive idea of being entitled to exploit others requires one to have a capacity to consider the justified claims of others. This can be induced by techniques of time progression, such as: "Do you want to be remembered as an arrogant and selfish tyrant?" or "What would you like to have written on your tombstone?"

Another frequent problem that occurs in the systemic interactions of families is parentification, which was first described by Boszormenyi-Nagy and Spark (1984) and which means that one or several children take over the parental role. Though this reverses the usual roles and can be seen as a violation of generation boundaries, it is not always a damaging situation for the child. The important point is whether the demands on the child are fair, regarding the circumstances, and whether the efforts are acknowledged. For example, a man has affairs, he finally divorces, and his wife gets depressed. The youngest daughter gets the responsibility of ensuring that the mother doesn't commit suicide. Even years later, when the daughter goes to a university in another city, she has to phone every evening to find out whether the mother is still alive and to calm her down. Twenty years later, the parentified daughter comes to therapy with severe depression after her own divorce. The therapist will acknowledge that she did not parentify her 15-year-old son. In the therapeutic relationship she changes between control and dependency, just as she had to behave toward her mother.

Coalitions or alignments are another problem issue in therapy and can be overt or subtle and hidden. They can impair individuation when generational boundaries are not respected, a constellation that Minuchin (1974) called "pathological triangulation." Circular questioning is quite an effective way of finding out where hidden coalitions are and how they work. Boszormenyi-Nagy and Spark (1984) were the first to describe loyalty as one of the most powerful drives in families. Loyalty can be understood as the link between the expectations of the family, on one hand, and the feelings and thoughts of the individual, on the other hand. Psychic structure can largely be understood as a process of loyal internalization of the expectations and the rules of the family. This process of loyal internalization can help us to understand delegation. Mild forms of delegation are universal, like a son taking over the business of his father or graduating in the profession his father had longed for but could not attain due to the war. Pathological delegations can happen when a child dies in a dysfunctional family that is incapable of dealing with loss. In this situation, the power of loyalty and delegation can force a sibling to continue the life of the deceased. This sibling will have difficulties developing his own personality and relating in an emotionally deep and satisfying way. Difficulties like drinking too much, severe depression, or suicide attempts can be the result years later. Delegation can be combined with family myths, secrets, and attributions.

When family loyalty is an issue, the psychotherapist is wise to proceed cautiously. When a family secret or a lie is torn away without mercy, a person may be exposed to shame, the regulation of self-esteem breaks down, and the person may get out of control and even commit suicide. It is much better to discuss the pros and cons of talking about family secrets together with the family. Here, circular questions can be quite helpful.

A MODEL FOR SYSTEMIC INTERVENTIONS FROM A CONTEXTUAL PERSPECTIVE

Each family is different and is usually quite a complex system. Models try to reduce complexity and to help the therapist understand the family system more quickly. No model can be free from basic assumptions, but these should be open to empirical and scientific research to determine whether these assumptions can be validated. So, a good model can offer chances for understanding and can give guidelines for treatment. We should also keep in mind that all theories, including family models, are ideas and concepts—on one hand, they help us to understand and intervene; on the other hand, we tend to observe what we believe, a self-fulfilling prophecy.

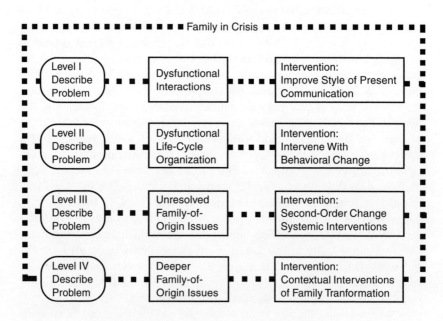

FIGURE 4.1. Modified Table of Jellouschek

Jellouschek (1998) has introduced a model for systemic couple therapy. This approach, based on Berne's transactional psychoanalysis, can be enlarged for family therapy and used in our contextual framework as well. As contextual therapists, we have a clear strategic orientation of moving a family away from suffering and dysfunctional behavior. This includes understanding the symptoms or the actual crisis as a sign that further steps toward growth and development have to be made. Patients, couples, or families that we see are usually stuck in the present. Important parts of the past are often not quite understood or worked through. It is our job as psychotherapists to open that door toward the future by being willing to deal with these past issues. We notice that a patient or a family reaches the perspective of future when people start having goals, plans, and perspectives. The model that Jellouschek (1998) proposes in figure 4.1 can give us an idea of when to address topics of the present, the past, or the future. The first two levels describe a context of problems we can observe in the present, whereas Levels III and IV are rooted in the past.

Level I Interventions: Dysfunctional Interactions

In this level, many times the family or a specific relationship is troubled because the interaction itself is troubled. In the contextual model, dysfunctional interactions may always represent deeper issues that deal with biological factors, individual psychology, or ethical concerns. The system, however, often produces a variety of problems because of the nature of interaction. We see a variety of systemic patterns that tends to be characteristic of dysfunctional relationships, such as misunderstandings in communications of relating and meaning, ingrained family patterns, symptoms that promote a benefit, and interactive solutions that perpetuate problems.

Communication of Relating and Meaning

Watzlawick (1967) and others have described classic situations where communication is used to promote relating but is understood as a rational effort. For example, a daughter tells what happened at school in her social relationships with boys. She wants emotional support from the father and reassurance that she has qualities that will help her be successful in relationships. However, her father tries rational problem solving by telling the daughter that she needs to do her hair differently or how to strike up conversations with boys. He may even do this in a critical manner. If this is the case, the daughter will feel misunderstood and will likely cry. The father, on the other hand, will likely be confused and frustrated that his efforts are not acknowledged.

Other possibilities of misunderstanding can be due to a lack of social skills or of clear communication, or perhaps there is no exchange about ideas and interpretation. Whenever the psychotherapist notices dysfunctional interactions, these should be addressed. This can be done by asking questions, telling stories, exaggerating the pattern, or giving interpretations and explanations. By the therapist doing so, the family can become less dysfunctional. Seeing the family change toward more communication and better understanding will stimulate hope and will strengthen the therapeutic alliance.

Ingrained Family Patterns

It is not unusual for any systemic relationship to develop a pattern that becomes an ingrained sequence that may be dysfunctional. Some of these patterns are well recognized in the literature. Hargrave (2000) has described some of these typical relational styles. When rigid polarization of these patterns occurs, conflicts or issues are difficult to resolve because the interactional pattern serves as a role structure that the relational partners perform. The pattern must be undone before there is any real hope of confronting the issue. He described couple exercises (Hargrave, 2000), in order to help partners identify and understand their most polarized patterns, as shown in figure 4.2. Instead of escalating fights, as both polarized individuals usually feel they are "right" and must convince and change their partner, they can step outside themselves and look at the way in which the interaction and the patterns of the conflict take place. The psychotherapist can then suggest new ways to deal with the pattern that will interrupt the escalation of conflict. These patterns can be observed in families as well. Just as is suggested for couples, all family members can indicate directly or by circular questioning where each family member is situated on a polarization continuum.

Interactions or Symptoms as Beneficial

Haley (1987) and Madanes (1981) are well-known strategic therapists and have long understood the meaning of symptomology as being controlled by the relational partners. With this understanding, many interactions or symptoms that seem dysfunctional or unwanted may contain benefit for at least one relational partner. For instance, a woman

Need for Intimacy

Concerning the need for intimacy, those with high needs for intimacy tend to pursue people to meet their intimacy needs. Those who have low needs for intimacy tend to distance from people to meet their need for separateness.

Distancer |————————————————————————| Pursuer

Getting Things Done

Those with high tendencies to "do" are overfunctioners, whereas those with tendencies to let others take care of details are underfunctioners.

Overfunctioner |————————————————————| Underfunctioner

Dealing with Change

Those who deal with change by relying on strong leadership and rules are more rigid. Those who deal with change in a laid-back and passive manner are more chaotic.

Rigid |————————————————————————————| Chaotic

Problem Solving

Those who try to solve problems by confrontation and hard work are aggressive. Those who try to avoid problems or to ignore issues that cause problems are avoiding.

Aggressive Style |——————————————————————| Avoiding Style

Dealing with Conflict

Those who are dogmatic and demanding in conflicts are blaming, whereas those who allow themselves to be dictated to during conflicts are placating.

Blaming |——————————————————————————| Placating

Activity of Intimacy

Those who are more apt to find intimacy in emotions are feeling-oriented, whereas those who find intimacy in activities are thinking-oriented.

Feeling Style |————————————————————————| Thinking Style

FIGURE 4.2. Typical Polarized Relational Patterns

may have a symptom of always having a headache that just will not go away. Although the headache may be very real, it also serves her well because it keeps her from having to be sexually intimate with her husband. In another example, a child's acting-out behavior at school may allow the parents to focus on an acceptable problem, instead of focusing on their conflicts and lack of intimacy. When a symptom or an interaction serves to benefit the system, the relational partners may not be aware of the importance of the symptom. However, the interaction must be changed in order to facilitate family and relational growth.

Many strategic techniques are useful in changing these interactions. One technique often employed by Madanes (1984) is to change the benefit of the symptom. For example, the following is from a case where the psychotherapist believed that a child's acting-out behavior was being used to keep the parents' focus on him exclusively.

Therapist: So, every time your son gets in trouble at school, what happens?

Mother: One of us usually have to drop whatever we are doing and go get him. When the other gets home, we have these endless discussions with him about the consequences of his behavior and why he does these things.

Therapist: Does it do any good?

Husband: Obviously not. We are here.

Therapist: Then I would like you to try a new strategy. I can see how your son's behavior has taken a toll on the marriage relationship. When he acts out, I would like the two of you to get away for a bit so you can get some relaxation from all the tension. Maybe something like this. When he acts out at school, go get him, but then whoever picks him up will arrange for a baby-sitter so the two of you can go out for dinner and a movie. I believe that when you get this kind of separation from your son, you two will make better decisions about what to do about his misbehavior in the morning.

After the couple employed the practice twice over the next 2 weeks, the son started proclaiming that he did not want his parents to leave him. The father responded, "We have to leave. It is what the therapist told us to do and we are going to follow her instructions. If you don't want us to leave, don't get in trouble." The result was that the boy acted out at school only one time during the next 60 days.

Other strategic techniques that have clinical success in dealing with symptomology or dysfunctional patterns include reframing ("Your wife is not nagging you, she just wants you to take care of yourself so you will live a long life."), relabeling ("Your husband is not trying to avoid you by working; rather, he wants you to have nice things."), prescribing the symptom ("Instead of trying to avoid a conflict, try to have one each time you have a meal."), offering descriptions ("Your son is to be commended for his acting out. It allows the two of you to avoid all the issues in the marriage and focus on him."), and predicting relapse ("Things seem to be getting better, so probably you will have a blowup this next week."). All of these interventions serve to throw off the system's normal functioning around the symptom or the interaction and require the relationship to challenge the benefits it derives from the symptomology (Madanes, 1981). From a contextual perspective, undermining the symptomatic interaction allows the relational issues to be dealt with in a more constructive manner.

Level II Interactions: Dysfunctional Life-Cycle Organization

Families have much stability. Some patterns, cognitions, and delegations are even passed on, over and over, for generations. On the other hand, there is always change when a couple marries, children are born, members grow older, and family members leave the house or die. So permanent change and transition also occur in families. Times of transition require flexibility, energy for change, and a capacity for coping with a new situation. But change, separation, and conflict between generations seem very dangerous to some families, and all the resistances mentioned previously can be mobilized. The result can be a family organization that has turned dysfunctional, because it hasn't changed according to the life cycle. Such parents might treat their grown-up children as if they were teens or might stop the 25-year-old daughter from having dates and moving away. But such a situation of enforced stability against the life cycle cannot last forever, and, usually, symptoms or problems will arise. For instance, a daughter may develop anorexia or one of the parents might have an affair.

In systemic thinking, these problems can be seen as information that a further step of personal development has to be accomplished. Therapeutic interventions on this level can use the experience of behavioral therapy, which includes detailed homework. This type of intervention is particularly appropriate when the members of the family or the relationship recognize the problems and know what solutions they should be actualizing but find it difficult to follow through. The psychotherapist can carefully instruct and utilize follow-up to help the relational members successfully form new habits that counteract old problems.

On a systemic level, the primary focus of the psychotherapist needs to be on removing the barriers that prevent the system from changing and on reorganizing the system. One of the many ways to reorganize the system is to utilize a structural family therapy approach (Minuchin & Fishman, 1981). Although a variety of techniques are used in this approach, one that is extraordinarily useful is the psychotherapist unbalancing the system by forming new boundaries or coalitions. For instance, the following is from a therapy session where the 22-year-old daughter kept intervening with her parent's relationship because she believed that the father did not treat the mother correctly.

Daughter: (To the father) You just don't realize how you constantly put Mom down. You are totally unreasonable.

Therapist: You seem to be the protector of your mother. (Looking at the mother) Do you need your daughter to protect you?

Mother: It feels nice to have someone take up for me.

Therapist: I'm sure that it does. Would you rather have someone take up for you or would you rather be emotionally close to someone?

Mother: I guess I would rather be close. I can take care of myself.

Therapist: Then I guess you would need to start taking care of yourself with your husband so you can eventually be close to him.

Daughter: (To the therapist) You don't understand how he berates her verbally.

Therapist: I know that you have been used to taking care of your mother. But it is time for you to move on with your life and let your parents either resolve their issues or break up. You can't be the one that takes up for your mother anymore.

Mother: (To the daughter) He's right, honey. I have to take on your father myself. You have your life to live. (Long pause and then to the father) We have to deal with our own issue ourselves.

Here the psychotherapist drew a boundary between the mother and the daughter that made it clear that if the mother refused to take care of herself in her relationship with her husband, it would mean that the daughter would be stuck in the family of origin. Given the choice, the mother moved to form a new coalition with her husband against the daughter, which, in the end, would serve the daughter well because it would move the family along the developmental cycle. Another effective structural technique (Minuchin & Fishman, 1981) is for the psychotherapist to use his or her expertise and power to reorganize the structure. For instance, in the previous example, when the daughter countered the boundary that was being drawn between her and her mother ("My mother needs me to take up for her"), the psychotherapist used his skill and power as an "expert" to tell the daughter that she must move on.

Some techniques from a solution-focused approach (deShazer, 1985) are effective in producing change as well. In the solution-focused approach, the psychotherapist wants to shift the focus of attention away from the problem—away from the feelings of being hopeless and helpless to ones of strength and power. DeShazer (1985) introduced several techniques to find solutions that can be used as well in our contextual framework of inducing change. For instance, giving compliments that make sense to the family instead of seeing only symptoms and disorder. Compliments and a recognition of strengths can help family members to establish a working alliance and to acknowledge their own resources.

One of the more dynamic tools of the solution-focused approach is the miracle question (deShazer, 1985). The miracle question is quite a powerful tool to shift the focus of attention away from the problem and to move a patient or a family toward a solution. The miracle question has the power to reorganize relational and problem thinking. For instance:

Suppose (pause) . . .	(Shift the attention to possibilities other than the "common suffering.")
you walk out of the therapy room, drive home, have supper, watch TV, and so on, and go to bed.	(Create and describe a context of everyday life.)
While you sleep, a miracle happens (pause) and your problem disappears just like this.	(Problem solving does not have to take years.)
But the miracle happened during your sleep and you don't know that your problem is gone.	(Intensive focusing on how the solution would feel.)

Would there be some change in
your body? How would your
partner notice that the problem
is gone?

How would your children notice?   (Differences in interaction.)
What would be different at work?
How would your friends and
colleagues find out?

(Pause) And what else?   (Consequence of change.)

    Before or after the miracle question, it is possible to introduce a
scale (like the subjective units of discomfort scale) and to ask the
patient or the family where they situate themselves between zero and
10, depending on how much or how little the problem causes problems or discomfort. Introducing such a scale offers a good opportunity to find out who in the family suffers most. Why does one family
member suffer less? What would have to happen in order to make the
situation one degree worse or one degree better? Having asked the
miracle question, the psychotherapist may continue the process of
inducing change by asking for exceptions. For example, the psychotherapist may ask, "When did something similar to the miracle last
happen?" Usually, a patient or a family can find examples, and it is
important to find out why these examples are not acknowledged. The
answers often lead to destructive circles of interaction and reveal
strengths that can be used to reorganize the structure of the relationships.

    Circular questioning (Selvini-Palazzoli, Boscolo, Cecchin, & Prata,
1978) also offers chances for the reorganization of developmentally
frozen patterns or relationships. Even difficult topics like sexual problems in couples' therapy can be addressed by using circular questioning. Usually, the members of the couple or the family are quite
astonished to find out that the other members know much more about
their personal needs and problems than everybody assumed. This
produces change toward more closeness and understanding. Circular
questioning should be practiced as long as necessary, because the
therapist has to be sure that everybody really listens. Even in difficult
families, circular questioning is quite a safe way for the therapist to
induce change because the family gets a chance to exchange views or
attributions. Traits of character or styles of behavior are often seen in

quite an arbitrary way, which is usually taken for granted and not discussed. Thus, circular questioning can open a door toward a shared reality construction of the family that can be more suitable.

Level III Interventions: Unresolved Family-of-Origin Issues

The last two levels of intervention are primarily aimed at the deep issues of love and trust that involve the individual psychology and relational ethics dimensions. Most of the intervention techniques used in these dimensions are discussed in detail in chapters 6 and 7.

As psychotherapists, we will always ask ourselves why and where a family is stuck and cannot change. Very similar to Hargrave's model of polarized patterns of interaction mentioned previously, Jellouschek (1998) has suggested three basic polarities for his work with couples, which can be adapted for families as well. These polarities are themes that life imposes. Polarities are natural, and even being on one extreme need not be avoided. Problems arise only when a person is rigidly stuck for years or decades at the same polar position. These polarities can be described as:

Autonomy vs. Bonding. These drives have been discussed already as centripetal and centrifugal forces. This polarity of autonomy versus bonding and quick change between the extremes can best be observed in adolescents. Extreme autonomy can be felt as isolation; too much bonding can seem like enmeshment or fusion.

Ordering vs. Giving In. As has already been discussed, this polarity of power for the individual is vital to survival; circular questioning can be helpful to find out how power issues are handled in a family.

Give-and-Take. This polarity of emotional exchange is one of the basics of contextual therapy and trustworthiness. It can be seen as a result of fair giving and receiving.

It is helpful for the psychotherapist to get an answer on how these polarities are handled in the family. Sometimes this will become clear after the first steps of regulation and of establishing the working alliance that has been made and when the family talks about its problems. Often, however, more detailed questions are necessary. When the therapist addresses the topics of losses, family secrets, and myths, it is very important to respect family loyalties. Myths are family attributions and should not be attacked. It can be more helpful to insert new perspectives or interpretations into the family system in a more indirect way, such as by telling a story or a joke about the pattern at stake. For instance, the following is from a therapy session where a young adult son was trying to make a decision concerning a career direction.

Man: My father was an accountant, and I know that he has always had the expectation that I would become an accountant and take over his business eventually.

Therapist: Has he ever told you this directly?

Man: Not directly. He just says things like it is a good stable business. It is a good career. Things like that.

Therapist: It sounds as if you respect your father for making a good business.

Man: That's true. He has been a great provider and a hard worker.

Therapist: I wonder if both of you have to have you be an accountant and take over the business to confirm those thoughts and feelings. In other words, in order to feel like you respect your dad and for him to feel your affection, you have to do the same thing he has done.

Man: (Long pause) I bet that some of that is true. That seems a little crazy, doesn't it?

Therapist: Well, it seems worthwhile. But I would think that you two might want to at least consider having a direct conversation about respect and care, instead of your having to dedicate 50 years of work to prove it.

Another technique that is used at this level is directing the members of the relationship to balance the give-and-take in the interactions (Hargrave & Anderson, 1992). Balancing give-and-take means that the psychotherapist analyzes the patterns of giving and receiving that take place in relating and identifies any imbalances that perpetuate distrust and dysfunction in the family interactions. For instance, an elderly mother may expect her daughter to care for her because she once cared for her elderly mother. However, the mother may be in good health and may be perfectly able to take on more giving to her daughter and her grandchildren. Balances in give-and-take perpetuate intergenerational family trust. The psychotherapist, therefore, can offer direction on how to recognize past giving in such a way that will allow the relational members to not just follow old patterns and justifications but to allow a strengthening of trustworthy giving to one another.

Level IV Interventions: Deeper Family-of-Origin Issues

Unresolved family-of-origin issues usually confront us with severe violations of love or trust. In these situations, systemic interventions are not sufficient to produce change or healing. The psychotherapist must look into the relational resources of the family in order to start a transformation process away from destructive actions to ones that are constructive. This difference between *intervention* and *transformation* may seem subtle, but in reality the difference lies in the intensity of the severe violation that has been perpetuated from one generation to the next. Of course, most of these violations deal with the relational ethics dimension and usually involve profound violations that cause deep pain, such as sexual abuse, murder, neglect, suicide, emotional rejection, or repudiation of relationships.

Although specific transformation techniques will be discussed later, it is important for the psychotherapist to remember that even the most severe of family violations occurred in the context of systemic interactions. Interactions are the medium of communication for love and trust. Therefore, it is possible for the psychotherapist to tap into these deep violations with very simple questions concerning the systemic reality of the relationships. For instance, "How did you know as a child that you were loved?" "What did you have to do as a child so that everything was okay?" "Can you remember an example—actual or many years ago— when your mother/father/your spouse was an emotional help for you?" These questions may get systemic interaction answers, but they also reveal the deep emotional underpinnings of damage to the elements of love and trust.

The issues that are involved at Level IV are complex because the emotional transgressions of the past may have shaped current interactions in such a way that even if the interactions could be changed, the emotional pain would remain intact. The pain, therefore, always becomes a driving force to return to the damaging or dysfunctional interactions. Transformations at this level demand sensitivity on the part of the psychotherapist to timing and partiality to the intergenerational framework. Some of the techniques that are used are multidirected partiality (Boszormenyi-Nagy & Krasner, 1986), understanding and choice (Hargrave, 1994), forgiveness and reconciliation (Hargrave, 2001), rituals that promote healing (Hargrave, 1994), and societal redressing of past events that were damaging.

Final Thoughts on Systemic Change

As biology and evolution teach us, life is a permanent process of adaptation and change. These processes of change can be gradual, almost unnoticed, and easy, or they can be abrupt and can demand much energy. Change can be cognitive and can produce a different understanding of a situation. Change can be emotional and can promote different feelings. Change can be behavioral and produce very different actions. But no matter what the context of change is, it takes place within an interactive format. Most psychotherapists who are familiar with the contextual therapy approach believe that it is simply a theory dealing with family-of-origin issues. Although it is true that some of the more original aspects of the approach deal with intergenerational issues, it is essential to remember our integrative stance. Intergenerational trust and love do not occur in a vacuum. They are produced, perpetuated, and communicated through the cognitions, emotions, and behaviors that take place in the interactive reality. As such, systemic interactions and understanding how to produce change in those interactions will always be essential to contextual therapists.

CHAPTER 5

The Drive to Be Constructive or Destructive

In many ways, the dimension of relational ethics can be thought of as a bridge from one's past, stretching through oneself to the future. The way that the bridge reaches into the past tells us much about who we are, what we deserve, and what we are obligated to give. This bridge back to the past may be a strong and trustworthy structure that provides stability for our being and our actions, or it may be weak and unsure, leaving us to question almost every part of our self-conceptions and interactions. But whether the bridge is strong or weak, it provides us with an undeniable link to our past. It is our legacy, heritage, and foundation. It impacts us cognitively, socially, emotionally, behaviorally, and spiritually. It is from this past that we make our contribution to the structure of how life is to be lived through the way we handle and deal with our relationships. No matter what their past, individuals become responsible for their part in the here and now, in making the bridge that runs through them either stronger or weaker.

What is most stirring about the fourth dimension of contextual therapy, however, is that the bridge moves from us into the future. Our work, actions, emotions, contributions, distractions, and destructiveness all become part of the legacy, heritage, and foundation that we pass along to others. These "others" may be part of our biological family relationships or may be part of the people whom we have made family by our commitments and love. But these people will be affected by our additions, either good or bad, to the complex bridge that we call life. Even if we have no sense of spirituality in terms of an afterlife or a supreme being, we must acknowledge that our influence on relationships makes part of us transcendent in terms of our effect on the next and future generations.

It is this fact that makes the dimension of relational ethics so powerful in human relationships. It amplifies all of what is true, both positive and negative, about the love and the trust that exist in my relationships with others. This information exists inside of me as I try and determine the best way to reconcile these deep drives to attain what I want and deserve with the desire to be responsible in my relationships. The choices that I make, in turn, will be amplified to even more relationships throughout my generational lineage. It is essential, therefore, that we understand how this dimension of relational ethics works and how we can utilize its power in the therapeutic setting.

ESSENTIAL ELEMENTS IN THE DIMENSION OF RELATIONAL ETHICS

The Resource of Trustworthiness

Trustworthiness in relationships is consistently identified as the most important resource in contextual family therapy (Boszormenyi-Nagy & Krasner, 1986; Goldenthal, 1996; Van Heusden & Van Den Eerenbeemt, 1987). It is important, however, to have an understanding of how trustworthiness becomes such an important resource. In order to understand, we must first discuss the underpinnings of trustworthiness, which are balance and justice.

Buber (1958) would maintain that we, as human beings, are dependent upon relationships in order to experience self-understanding and self-awareness. This interaction demands that at a minimum, two parties participate. As we interact, we possess an innate sense of justice that demands that as we give our interactions to the other in relationship, we are entitled to receive something from the interactions of the other. This process describes justice at its most essential form. When we balance what we are entitled to receive from relationships and what we are obligated to give in order to maintain relational existence, we have satisfied our innate drive toward justice. As we mentioned previously, we are entitled in every relationship to take something for ourselves and are obligated to give something back to the other person. The give-and-take in relationship has to be balanced so that our sense of justice or fairness is upheld.

It is the *relational ethic* that drives us to take responsibility for achieving some form of fairness in the process of give-and-take (Hargrave, Jennings, & Anderson, 1991). As previously stated, when we are involved in a relationship where the obligations and entitlements are balanced, our sense of justice is satisfied and trust results. We come to trust the relationship to provide us with what we are entitled to, so we simply do not have to worry about being denied what we deserve. This trustworthiness, therefore, works as a resource for us and allows us to concentrate on how we give to the relationship. This giving earns us merit or entitlement. *Entitlement is the ethical claim to receive compensation that we have in any relationship where we have given or contributed in a responsible and reliable fashion* (Boszormenyi-Nagy & Krasner, 1986). Our giving, in turn, builds the amount of trustworthiness our relational partners have in us and gives them the freedom to concentrate on their giving. In these types of relationships, there is a spiral of growth, as trustworthiness increases and relational partners have no need to manipulate or threaten the other into giving. *Trustworthiness, then, is the relational resource that accrues on the side of a reliable, responsible, and considerate partner who justly gives what she or he is obligated to provide in the relationship* (Boszormenyi-Nagy & Krasner, 1986).

Relationships have an important quality, above and beyond the individuals who participate in them. Relationships are, in a sense, living and breathing beings (Hargrave, 2000). For instance, when spouses engage in a relationship, there are three relational considerations: each spouse as an individual and their relationship together. This living being that is the "relationship together" was called by Carl Whitaker "us-ness" or "we-ness." It is clear that even though a couple's relationship is in many way invisible, it takes on a personality of its own and has its own likes and dislikes. When a couple acts in trustworthy ways, the partners' relational "us-ness" is strengthened and becomes vital. It informs the spouses about intimacy, growth, nurture, and warmth. It is, by nature, made up of the two spouses but is more than the sum of the two individuals (Hargrave, 2000).

As contextual therapists, we believe that it is not only necessary for the psychotherapist to be responsible for considering the best outcomes for the individuals involved, it is also necessary for him or her to give due consideration to the relationship. The relationship, not just the individuals, perpetuates care for others in spousal and friendship connections, but especially in familial relations that exist between successive generations. Contextual therapy is not simply another theory on how to help individuals. It posits that relationships have their own identities and deserve due consideration, just as much as do the individuals who participate in the relationships (Hargrave, 2000). As such, it is not just individuals who are dependent upon love and trustworthiness; relationships are kept alive by the same resources.

Deterioration of Trust, Destructive Entitlement, and the Revolving Slate

In a previous chapter, we illustrated a ledger of a balanced horizontal relationship between equals, such as the type that would exist between spouses. Of course, not all relationships build trustworthiness. Table 5.1 illustrates a relational ledger between spouses that is unfair and imbalanced. In this case, let us say that the wife is giving her husband respect, care, love, intimacy, nurture, financial commitment, and fidelity. In return, however, the husband provides none of these things. He is disrespectful and calls her obscene names. He hardly ever extends himself emotionally to her or cares for her feelings. In place of love, he often expresses disdain and disgust with her. Finally, in place of loving intimacy and fidelity, he carries on emotionally and physically with other women. As seen in the illustration, what the woman is entitled to take from the relationship is nonexistent. She is, simply stated, being cheated out of her just entitlement. In this kind of situation, trustworthiness evaporates. The woman, however, still will have the relational ethic drive toward balance and justice, which will require her action. What is she to do in order to achieve a balance between what she receives and what she has given? Most likely, she will take one of three actions in the relationship: withdrawal, threats, or manipulation.

The imbalance in the relationship causes a deep emotional reaction. The wife will likely become frustrated and angry because she is indeed being cheated. This is simply another illustration of how contextual therapists understand emotions. Emotions, in this dimension, are simply gauges that give us a reading of where we are in the balance of give-and-take in relationships. The wife feels provocative emotions because the balance of the relationship is thrown off. She

TABLE 5.1
Unfair Relational Ledger Between Husband and Wife

Merit or Take (What Individual Is Entitled To)	Obligations or Give (What Individual Is Obligated to Give)
	1. Respect 2. Care 3. Love 4. Intimacy 5. Nurture 6. Financial Responsibility 7. Fidelity

may decide that the relationship is hopeless and may separate from or divorce her husband. If she does, however, she will still likely carry injustice and accompanying emotions to other relationships. For instance, she may meet another man and may demand unreasonable promises from him before she proceeds in the relationship. She may develop a relationship and become hypervigilant because she is fearful of the person being sexually unfaithful. Even if she does not develop another relationship, she may take out her anger by expressing to her son, "You are just like your father" or to her daughter by saying, "You never can trust any man."

The wife in the previous illustration may stay in the relationship, but her feelings of anger and frustration that are rightly driven by the injustice may cause her to become threatening or manipulative. For instance, she may become verbally abusive of the husband. Also, she may take the financial resources that the couple has accumulated and hide them, threatening that he will be left "out in the cold" if he does not start behaving in the relationship. She may become manipulative, to try and get him to do his part in the relationship. For example, she may have an affair with another man herself, in order to make her husband feel jealous and start investing back into the relationship. The problem, of course, with these threats and manipulations is that even if the husband starts giving to the relationship, it will be a dissatisfying experience for both partners. The wife will have to wonder whether the husband really desires to give or he is just doing it because of her actions. The husband will feel the threats and the manipulation, and his giving will likely cause only resentment and anger on his part.

The withdrawal, manipulation, or threat from the wife is being driven by her sense of justice, but instead of the drive resulting in trustworthy giving, it results in her trying to secure entitlement for herself at a high cost. Instead of feeling the freedom to give to relationships, she feels the drive and the requirement to do whatever is necessary to get what she needs and to make sure that she is not taken advantage of again. These actions are called destructive entitlement. *Destructive entitlement means destructive actions or emotions that result from an individual's claim to self-justifying compensation for an unjust and unbalanced relational ledger* (Hargrave & Anderson, 1992).

It is important to note that as contextual therapists, we understand the drives of destructive entitlement but do not accept the practice of withdrawal, manipulation, or threats. Any type of destructive, vindictive, or manipulative action simply removes more trustworthiness from the relational reality and supplies the doer of the maladaptive behavior with little or no satisfaction. Even though the relational ethic is the source of the drive toward compensation, one never moves past the ethical requirement of taking responsibility for one's own actions. Stated in simple terms, an individual is never relieved of his or her responsibility to give in ethical, trust-building ways (Boszormenyi-Nagy & Krasner, 1986). To engage in destructive entitlement is to actively and irresponsibly take part in the destruction of trust and of relationships. Even if we are recipients of such damage, damaging others will simply ensure the perpetuation of more injustice and will likely damage innocent parties.

It is fairly simple to see how balance, justice, entitlement, and trustworthiness are achieved in *horizontal* relationships, or relationships between equals, because in any particular relationship what one gives, one is entitled to receive from the other. It is much more difficult to recognize how the balance is achieved in *vertical* relationships, or relationships between successive generations. These relationships, such as the ones that exist between parents and children, are by nature asymmetrical in give-and-take. For instance, table 5.2 is an example of a relationship ledger between a parent and an infant. The parent has much more obligation than the child has. The right side of the ledger shows a partial list of giving that the parent is obligated to provide. These include love, care, nurture, security, protection, and discipline to the child. However, there is no real entitlement or merit that the parent receives in return. This does not mean, of course, that the parent does not have expectations for the child to eventually be responsible and to give for the good of the family. The difference, however, is that the parent *has these expectations for the child's good.* These expectations for responsibility and giving on the child's part are not for the parent's benefit. Also, even if the child does not meet these expectations or fulfill the responsibility, the parent will still have the requirement of providing for the child. For instance, if the infant is a difficult child and often rejects the parent's efforts to cuddle and nurture, the parent is still obligated to continue to love and nurture the child. This is very different in horizontal relationships. If one spouse rejects the other, trust breaks down and the individuals will likely cease to function in a relationship. But in vertical relationships, the parent is obligated to care for and nurture the child, even if the child rejects the parent. This type of giving in the vertical relationship is trustworthy, even if the child is unresponsive. Almost instinctively, we would all agree that it is parents' responsibility to give not only far more than they receive from the child, but also that it is their responsibility to give to the child even if they receive

TABLE 5.2
Fair Relational Ledger Between a Parent and a Child

Parental Merit or Take From the Child (What the Parent Is Entitled To)	Parental Obligations or Give to the Child (What the Parent Is Obligated to Give)
Nothing	1. Love 2. Care 3. Nurture 4. Security 5. Protection 6. Discipline

nothing in return. This is the nature of vertical relationships (Hargrave & Anderson, 1992).

How can such a ledger be fair and balanced? In order to understand how it is fair, one must view the ledger from an intergenerational perspective. The vertical relationship is asymmetrical but fair, because it supposes that parents were once infants and were the beneficiaries of the same love, care, nurture, security, protection, and discipline that they are now expected to give to their infants. When the parents were children, they received the giving of their parents without the obligation to give it back to the parents. But as the parents grew to adulthood and had their own children, they now carried the obligation to balance the intergenerational ledger by giving care to their children. By fulfilling the obligation for such care to their infants, parents earn merit by obligating children to pass along such care to future grandchildren. In vertical relationships, therefore, balance and justice are maintained down through the succeeding generations. When individuals responsibly fulfill their obligations in a vertical relationship, they essentially empower the next generation to do the same. This giving provides an oscillating balance of give-and-take in the intergenerational group and produces the resource of trustworthiness. Trustworthiness, in turn, enhances and ensures the continued family existence and care for one another (Hargrave, 2001).

Of course, all families do not function in this manner. Many people have grown up in families where they, as children, were expected to care for the adults as if they, the children, were the parents. For instance, as seen in table 5.3, a parent may provide food and clothing to the child but may expect the child to make the parent feel loved, cared for, and nurtured. The child, because he or she is dependent upon the relationship with the parent and wants to please, will try to fulfill the request. This generational manipulation of obligations and

TABLE 5.3
Unfair Relational Ledger Between a Parent and Child

Parental Requirement From the Child (What the Parent Feels Entitled to Get)	Parental Give to the Child (What the Parent Feels Obligated to Give)
1. Love 2. Care 3. Nurture	1. Food 2. Clothing

entitlements is called *parentification, or the obligation the child feels from the parent to take on more responsibility than is age-appropriate* (Boszormenyi-Nagy & Spark, 1984). There are situations where it is functional for a child to take on additional family responsibilities, such as when a parent becomes ill or needs assistance. Parentification, however, occurs when children are deprived of their just entitlement and are required to give what they should receive from their parents. Such action is harmful to children and destroys trustworthiness in the intergenerational family.

Of course, children do not forget about this love, care, and nurturing that is owed to them. They have an innate sense of justice that drives them toward balanced obligations and entitlements. Therefore, when they grow up, they will seek to satisfy their drive for the just entitlement they deserve. Instead of seeking this entitlement from the parents who owed them, however, they will most likely try to get their entitlement from innocent parties. These innocent parties are most often their spouses or their children. Instead of having a foundation of trust resources and feeling the freedom and self-delineation necessary for giving, these adult children will likely feel justified in manipulating or demanding that their entitled needs be met through their spouses or their own children (Boszormenyi-Nagy & Spark, 1984). Like the parents many years before, their children will seek to meet these requirements. Inevitably, however, these children will fail to provide what the parents feel they deserve because they are ill equipped to give this type of love and nurture on an adult level. As the child fails, the parent will likely not relent in demanding his or her entitlement and most likely will become even more demanding and manipulative. Many times, the parent will even become abusive in an effort to get a child to fulfill the unfair obligation. The parent, when rational, may even feel badly about abusing the child. However, this drive is not so much a cognitive construct as it is an emotional one. The emotional drive causes a parent to feel *justified* in demanding that his or her deserved entitlement of love, care, and nurturing be met (Hargrave & Anderson, 1992). As is often the case in our clinical work, many abusive parents hate themselves for the terrible things they do to their children, yet they still feel justified in trying to get their needs met.

As damaged parents seek to secure their just entitlement, they are robbing the child of just entitlement. This produces the same injustices and distrust experienced by the parent in the next generation's experience. This is an intense cycle of destructive entitlement, because it originates in past generations and is passed along to the future in a ledger of distrust and injustice (Boszormenyi-Nagy & Spark, 1984). This cycle is called the *revolving slate, where one generation uses destructive entitlement to create new victims in the next generation* (Boszormenyi-Nagy & Krasner, 1986).

Where there are severe imbalances between this relational give-and-take, whether in horizontal or in vertical relationships, individuals will feel either cheated or overbenefited. Trust is drained, and the individuals in the relationship feel that their just entitlement is threatened or denied. Instead of people giving to one another in a trustworthy way, all of their relationships are prone to becoming arenas where individuals strive only to secure their own entitlement and to take care of themselves. The form of destructive entitlement can manifest in many ways. These might include paranoid attitudes, hostility, rage, emotional cutoff, and destructive harm to other individuals. The imbalances may promote destructive actions in a gradual manner, or the destructive entitlement may manifest itself in a single violent and destructive act. Destructive actions from a gradual decline in relational trustworthiness may be seen in behaviors such as erecting emotional barriers or engaging in consistent manipulation, emotional distance, or irresponsibility. Examples of more violent and destructive acts are retribution or revenge, consistent verbal attacks or threats, physical and sexual abuse, neglect, and addiction (Hargrave, 2001).

Loyalty, Invisible Loyalty, and Split Loyalty

Loyalty is not a bad thing, but it is very powerful. Loyalty is when an attachment in a relationship is preferred over another relationship (Boszormenyi-Nagy & Spark, 1986). This is appropriate in many ways and helps us understand priority and allegiance. For instance, most of the time a person will feel loyalty to the obligations and expectations of his or her family over those of friendships. A father who puts off plans to go to a sporting event with his friends in order to see his daughter perform in a school play is making an appropriate loyalty choice.

Loyalty is powerful in relationships because it essentially proclaims our priority and thereby suggests an organization or a hierarchy of how we will go about meeting obligations and receiving entitlements. Family loyalty is almost always expected and given because of the nature of family relationships. Because families are almost always the first relationships we experience, families have the intitial opportunity to program our constructs regarding our being and our actions toward relationships. Our initial beliefs concerning how lovable, worthy, and unique we are all depend upon those first formative family caretaking relationships. The same is true regarding our beliefs about the trustworthiness of relationships. No other time is so powerful in forming these constructs, by the simple fact that families offer the first time for these constructs to occur. Every other relationship, no matter how important to us, can never have this initial claim to helping us form our thoughts about who we are and how we are to act in relationships (Hargrave, 2001). The link, therefore, to our biological families is very strong, and our loyalty to that group usually follows. This loyalty serves as a link of trustworthiness to the family and to the intergenerational faith put forward to other generations.

There are many times, however, when loyalty can become a problem in relationships. When the family experiences destructive actions, it is not unusual for different family members to place competing obligations on family members. For instance, a divorcing husband and wife may hate one another. They may both say that the other does not meet their needs, the other is neglectful or hateful, and they do not love one another any more. These actions are, of course, destructive to their horizontal relationship but can be equally so in their vertical relationship with their children. If the mother, for instance, tells the children how awful and irresponsible their father is and that she cannot understand why the children would ever want to spend time with the father, the children are in a quandary. They are biologically created from both their mother and father, and both parents are important to them. But now the mother has put a demand on the children, which basically means, "If you are going to be loyal to me, you must reject your father." If the father responds to this attack through the children by accusing the mother of being evil and mean and instructs the children never to be like their mother, he places the children in an even more precarious position. The children will be placed in a position of *split loyalty*. Split loyalty is when *an individual is required to show loyalty to one deserving relationship at the cost of betraying or being disloyal to another deserving relationship* (Boszormenyi-Nagy & Krasner, 1986).

In the case of children, split loyalty is one of the most destructive forms of entitlement. Adults who place a child in this position are demanding that the child give an inappropriate obligation, which will likely cause parentification. But more seriously, the adult is requiring the child to reject the entitlements from other relationships, thereby cheating the child of what he or she justly deserves. The stress and the strain that split loyalty causes with children are most evident with divorcing parents who continue to engage in conflict. The result is not only a deterioration of trust but is also related to the child not doing as well academically, having a higher incident of delinquency, and having difficulty in future relationships (Amato & Booth, 1997).

Another common situation of split loyalty occurs within marriage. Many times, a family of origin will demand the loyalty of an adult son or a daughter at the expense of that son's or daughter's loyalty to a spouse. Sometimes, spouses refuse to give their loyalty to their partners because they prefer to be loyal to the family of origin. Again, this type of loyalty demand from the family of origin is a destructive violation of the trustworthiness that should exist in the intergenerational framework. It destablilizes the marriage and, developmentally, arrests the ability of the family to grow and procreate. For example, the following is from a case in which a woman was in a situation of split loyalty between her husband and her family of origin.

Husband: We can never make a financial move without you first checking it out with your parents. My God, I don't even have control over my own finances. Your parents control us.

Wife: They have lent us money before, and I think they have a right to have some involvement. Besides, it was because of the bad financial decisions you made that they had to get involved.

Husband: What are you saying? Are you saying that our financial problems are only because of me?

Wife: If you would have been more in control and made better decisions, we wouldn't be in the mess we are in.

Therapist: (To the wife) You have clear expectations of how he should have been more in control of the finances. Where did you form those ideas?

Wife: My father. He has told me from the beginning to keep an eye on my husband and what he does financially. My father was able to spot this problem from the very beginning.

Therapist: Does your father still tell you things like this?

Wife: All the time. I just wish I would have listened to him sooner. My father is right. He is going to end up having to support the two of us if I don't get out of this marriage.

Therapist: If your husband doesn't do it like your father says?

Wife: Yes.

In this case, the wife felt a split loyalty, in which being loyal to her father demanded that she be disloyal to the husband. Interestingly, she also placed her husband in a double bind, whereby she was demanding that he be in control of the finances and also that he listen to her and her father and do what they say. Split loyalty is always inappropriate and is the result of an irresponsible relational member making a destructive entitlement demand on an individual who should be free to pursue multiple relationships.

The last type of loyalty that concerns us here is invisible loyalty. *Invisible loyalty* was a term coined by Boszormenyi-Nagy and Spark (1984) to explain why some individuals engage in seemingly unreasonable behavior. Many times, an individual comes from a family where the revolving slate has injustices that are so severe and so numerous, it is difficult to distinguish any clear identity. The individual is tied to the family because of the previously mentioned power, but the demands of the family's destructive entitlement on the individual has left him or her with what seems to be an endless and unfulfilled list of obligations. These situations can be so destructive as to cause individuals to give up themselves as pawns who must sacrifice individuality in order to meet the demands of the family. This type of loyalty is driven by the destructive entitlement of family members and the innate desire of the individual to be loved and trusted by the family. *Invisible loyalty, therefore, is indirect action by a victim of destructive entitlement to fulfill unjust obligations in an effort to gain love and regard from the family of origin.*

These invisible loyalty actions may be directed toward others in relationships or may be directed toward self-destructive behavior. For instance, consider a man who refuses to have children with his wife because he was physically abused by his parents. In this case, the man received a strong covert message from his parents that their lives would have been better had they not had children. He later admitted his fear that if he had children, not only would he receive their anger because there would be more children brought into the family, but he would carry the same resentment toward his children that his parents had for him. Split loyalty is also seen in self-destructive patterns, such as addiction or psychosomatic illness (Cotroneo & Krasner, 1977). For instance, the following is from a case in which a woman was struggling with sexual promiscuity and drug addiction.

Therapist: Do you have any sense of what drives you to seek refuge in sexual relationships or drugs?

Woman: I just know that I can't stand to be around my mother. I want to get away from her nagging.

Therapist: Yet you live with your mother.

Woman: Yeah. I guess that sounds funny even when I say it. The thing is, my mother is the closest thing I have. I have always depended on her. I think she also depends on me.

Therapist: In what way?

Woman: My father divorced my mother when I was 3. I remember the day he left. From that time on, I always remember my mother talking in "we." "We are going to be okay. We are having financial difficulties. We are going to school." She would talk in "we," even though it was supposed to be my college education or her job.

Therapist: So your mother has to have you?

Woman: I know that this sounds crazy because I'm in such a mess, but I'm really the one who keeps my mother together. If she had to face her own stuff, she would go crazy.

Therapist: So the sex and drugs are really tied up with a great sacrifice on your part. It keeps you a mess so that your mother can take care of you and keep her life together.

Woman: I know it sounds crazy, but I swear that is what's going on.

Like any loyalty, invisible loyalty is extremely powerful. As contextual therapists, we find it a difficult balance to interrupt a destructive invisible loyalty while still allowing the individual to remain loyal. Cutting off an invisible loyalty might plunge an individual into excessive shame or guilt because he or she might feel like a traitor to the family or feel irresponsible in fulfilling obligations. The destructiveness, however, of invisible loyalty will certainly destroy people's efforts at future relationships and may result in their destroying themselves. It is necessary, therefore, to undo this destructive form of loyalty.

RELATIONAL ETHICS AND THERAPEUTIC CHANGE

The dimension of relational ethics has received very little exploration in the field of psychology (Van Heusden & Van Den Eerenbeemt, 1987), not because there is some conspiracy or ignorance in looking at these issues. It has not been dealt with in depth simply because this dimension poses significant problems when it comes to addressing dysfunction. First, there is the issue of the intergenerational nature of the dimension. If there is indeed a revolving slate that is passed from one generation to the next and the injustices that are experienced in one generation are passed to the next, the pathology is not as simple as designating a "good guy" and a "bad guy." The reality that victimizers are most often victims first requires our attention. We cannot do individual psychotherapy with an individual who struggles with his or her self-concept or destructive actions by simply blaming things on the immediate previous generation. From a contextual perspective, each generation has claims of entitlements, obligations, manipulation, and threats from the previous generation. Most psychotherapists deal only with the generation of people that consist of their patients, or, at most, they include one other generation in their assessments or interventions. Contextual therapists must constantly look at the formation of individuality, the consequences of actions, and the responsibility for the future through the lens of at least a three-generational complex. Therefore, the contextual therapist has to be willing to work and make interventions with the past, present, and future in mind at all times. There are victims, just as there are victimizers. But because most of the time these two roles exist in the same individual, we recognize that the intergenerational nature of this dimension demands our partiality and our sensitivity to people and to ledgers of history, as well as to the future.

Second, injustices pose difficulty in terms of intervention. Many of our traditional therapeutic routes are cut off if we are aware of the relational ethics dimension. The humanistic perspective in psychology has been one of the major driving forces in psychotherapy, as well as in Western culture. Most psychotherapists are well aware of the value of improving patients' self-images and moving individuals along the path to their own self-actualization. All too often, however, this has been interpreted by individuals and by the psychotherapeutic community to mean that people should do what satisfies themselves and makes them happy (Hargrave, 2000). Individuals do deserve consideration, but not at the expense of other relationships or other individuals. We remember a situation in group counseling several years ago in which a man who recently "came out" decided to stay with his wife and his two children. He was chastised by several group members because he was unwilling "to be himself" or was "selling himself out." On the contrary, this man simply made his decision by taking into consideration what would be best for him, his wife, their marriage, and their children. The popular notion that we can encourage people to pursue their happiness or self-growth at the expense of others is simply not possible if we pay attention to this fourth dimension. Happiness, freedom, responsibility, obligations, and peace are dependent upon multiple considerations.

Also, our interventions that are directed at simple behavioral change or reframing may be diluted. Behaviors that seem to be good for one person may not be good for another. For instance, a man who has difficulty with handling stress may become depressed. We may find out that his depression lifts when he spends time with friends, riding motorcycles. Our temptation is to prescribe the simple behavioral change to ride motorcycles more. However, the behavioral change that might be good for him may be a disaster for his wife and his family, who are desperate for his attention or affection. Likewise, we often seek to reframe people's interpretation of relationships and actions in order to give them another perspective on reality. Although there are appropriate uses of reframing when it recognizes the relational ledger concerns of others, reframing is inappropriate when it discounts an individual's perception of the emotional field of the intergenerational family. For instance, a psychotherapist may carelessly reframe a man's interpretation that his father never spent time with him as the father's attempt to make his son more independent. Such a reframe denies an emotional fact that the man carries with him, no matter what the specifics of his father's actions were. If the psychotherapist serves the emotional field, the man is likely to regard the psychotherapist with distrust and be wary of any change that is attempted.

Finally, there is the difficult issue of pain. Destructive entitlement, violations of love and trust, and the revolving slate all result in individuals carrying real emotional pain. As people come to the painful realization that the family members who are obligated to care for them cannot be trusted, they internalize the emotional trauma. Many times, individuals will interpret the violation of justice and trust as personal deficiencies, which result in internal shame. If the violation is severe, individuals are likely to internalize the experience that they are unloved or unlovable. This internalization delivers an intolerable blow to one's self-concept and image (Hargrave, 2001). As mentioned before, this can then manifest in an array of coping behaviors, which can include rage, shame, control, and chaos.

Pain, however, is a confusing construct to psychotherapists. There are times that we equate pain with the expression of emotion. We often feel that we are not successful at treatment unless we get the individual who is in pain to express it in some emotional catharsis. Also, the severity of pain is difficult to understand. Many times in our clinical work, we see an individual who experiences seemingly mild manipulation from the family of origin, yet appears to be an emotional wreck. On the other hand, there are times when we have seen a person who has been the victim of the most heinous kinds of physical and sexual abuse look very controlled and unaffected. We have made it our habit in clinical work not to try and judge pain. We realize that the person who looks "together" may be in as much or more pain than the individual who looks like a "wreck." This is because the origin of pain remains in the violation of love and trust. It doesn't really matter how love and trust were violated; pain will be the result. People will vary in their responses to pain, but where there is violation, there will be pain for relational members.

What is difficult for us and for many other psychotherapists to realize is that something needs to be done about the pain and that we are relatively powerless to address it directly. The essence of what people believe about themselves and about how to behave in relationships is formed by family members who took on enormous power because of their positions. We are simply psychotherapists and have no such position or power to alter people's internal software and rewrite their self-concepts and beliefs about relationships. We can certainly say that our patients are valuable, unique, and worthy, but almost without exception, they will not be able to integrate our words into beliefs if they have been taught something different by their families. The dimension of relational ethics forces us to deal with such pain and violations from a perspective of utilizing the people and the families that are powerful enough to address such pain. It forces us to deal with people who may still be destructive. It forces us to deal with the reality that pain must be used by the individual for growth, instead of the individual escaping the pain in order to grow. Pain is messy. The causes and solutions to pain, however, are far messier. We, as psychotherapists, have an important and powerful role to play in mobilizing the resources for healing and growth, but we cannot be the exclusive resource for healing and growth. By nature, relational ethics demand that the healing of pain must come from the powerful people who formed the legacy. This requires the inclusion of family members, whether or not they actually attend the therapy sessions.

The fourth dimension poses problems in therapy; however, there are far more strengths. First, by working in the fourth dimension psychotherapists are made aware of the second-order forces at work in the family psychology. As such, we speak and do therapy with issues that our patients readily recognize as "the heart of the matter" or the "real issue." Contextual therapists are dealing with the transcendent parts of individuals that are passed along through the generational lineage. In simple terms, contextual therapists are dealing with the family soul.

Second, there is enormous hope in the contextual framework. Each generation has an important role to play in either strengthening or weakening the intergenerational ledger. As such, each new generation has an opportunity to improve relationships and make individuals in the group feel loved and trusted. Likewise, in even the most painful and dysfunctional groups, a new starting point is offered to make the status of love and trust in the family better. This not only provides a hope for future family members to recover from a dysfunctional legacy but also gives an opportunity for people to get relief from their own painful legacy of violations.

Finally, the fourth dimension reforms the psychotherapist's impact. We most often think of ourselves as helping one individual or one family. We seldom think about the fact that as we work with individuals and families, we are also working with all the relationships in which those people participate. From a contextual perspective, the impact of psychotherapy is even broader. Successful therapy that addresses relational ethics affects the relationships in succeeding generations for as long as history lasts. We are reminded of a letter sent to one of us from a woman who was a patient, a year after she finished therapy:

> I had to write you and tell you an amazing story. I remember from our therapy that you encouraged me to recognize that I had worth and value and that what I did with my worth or value would have an effect on someone else. I didn't really believe that at the time, but now I do.
>
> As you know, I have been cut off from my daughter for years, and she asked me never to contact her again. I honored her wishes and decided that I would try to make some compensation for what I did to her by volunteering to do work at the Hospice. I really struggled with being at the Hospice, but I kept remembering the encouragement to recognize that I have worth and that I can communicate that worth to others. In one family I worked with, the mother was dying of cancer and her daughter had been estranged for several years because

the mother was abusive. The daughter said to me how she just couldn't face her mother and how angry she was. I told her that I understood, but I also understood her mother. I told her how I knew what it felt like to be in this mother's shoes—living your life in anger and resentment, hating yourself for things that you have done and said, wasting so much precious time—and that this was an opportunity to set it right. She asked me into the room with her and her mother and with one hand I reached for the daughter and with the other I reached for the mother. I don't know exactly how this came to me, but I remember us talking in therapy about the one thing I wanted to be remembered for. I said that we could each say one thing that we want to carry out from the room. The mother said that before she died, she wanted the daughter to know that she was sorry and that she loved her daughter. The daughter said that she wanted the mother to know that things were going to be okay. I said that if I ever got another chance with my own daughter, I would follow their example and not waste it on arguing or being defensive. I let go of their hands and they embraced and cried.

This had such a deep impact on me. I went home and cried for hours. I felt that I had done some good. But the real surprise came a week ago. I didn't know it and she didn't know it, but the daughter of this dying woman is an old friend of my daughter. She went to visit my daughter about two months after her mother died and told her this story about how the volunteer helped her and her mother get some healing and how glad she was that she had made that connection with her mother before she died. My daughter called me last week and said that when she heard her friend talk, she knew that she wanted to try and see if we could resolve our issues. I was stunned. I told my daughter that I was that volunteer. She couldn't believe it. I didn't even know her friend's last name and her friend didn't know me. After we got over the shock, we realized how important this opportunity was to get things right. Since last week, I have spoken with my daughter three times and am headed out to see her next month.

You never know what impact you can have and how things might come around. I am finally believing that I have some worth and value because I can give that to my daughter. Thank you.

Working in the dimension of relational ethics is actually a high privilege that we take seriously. It is mostly about the focus of assessing and understanding the intergenerational issues of love and trust with regard to the relational ledger. Current, past, and present consideration of all relational parties is all part of the complex work. Recognizing and blocking the dynamics of destructive entitlement are essential. But working in this dimension also involves mobilizing the strengths and resources that exist in the family. Even though these resources may be meager, any foundation can be used by the psycho-therapist to start a spiral of trustworthiness developing within the relationships. As mentioned before, because relational traumas in this dimension are deep and may have implications for generations to come, we see the work of the contextual therapist in this dimension better described as transformations, instead of interventions. Although we will discuss the primary transformation strategies in chapter 7, we will mention the ideas here with a brief description.

Right Script but Wrong Players

A friend and colleague, Glen Jennings, once described contextual therapy as people having the right script to act, but the wrong actors were present. In other words, it is impossible to perform the play *Othello* with the players of *Romeo and Juliet* (Hargrave, 1994). Many times, people take the relational ledger that existed with their families of origin and seek what they need from their spouses or children. The key idea in this strategy is to help patients recognize that they do have a legitimate relational claim, but that the people they are trying to claim the entitlement from are not equipped and are unable to meet the need. If possible, the psychotherapist will direct the patient back to the relational members who actually owe the patient entitle-ment. If relational redress is not possible, the psychotherapist helps the patient recognize the areas that stimulate the desire to pursue destructive entitlement and help to insulate innocent relationships from the effect.

Working Up and Working Down

One of the opportunities that exists within the dimension of relational ethics is that patients are simultaneously a part of different genera-tions. For instance, patients who are in their 40s most likely have parents or even grandparents alive and, at the same time, have chil-dren of their own. This places individuals in a context where they can clearly understand the giving-and-taking demands from the perspec-tive of both parent and child. Very often, it is difficult for individuals to indirectly address the relational violations that they have experi-enced or perpetrated directly. Working up and working down allow the psychotherapist to indirectly address these issues concerning the ledger, so as not to cause defensiveness or aggressiveness. The main idea with this technique is to focus on the needs or entitlements of either one generation up or one generation down, in order to help patients access the quandary of other relational members and look toward fulfilling their relational obligations. For instance, a psychotherapist may ask parents what they wanted from their mother and father at a certain age, in order to eventually make it clear that the parents have a similar obligation to their children.

Balancing Obligations and Entitlements

Many times in damaging families, untrustworthy and unloving actions have been perpetuated so long that the initial violations are no longer remembered. Instead, the relationship is "bad" because everyone is aware of how harmful it was in the past, and family members consistently speak about how awful and destructive interactions were. In most of these cases of long-standing violation, a belief, or a mythology dominates the current relationship. This means that the relational members no longer interact around give-and-take; instead, their interactions are totally dominated by the beliefs they have about each other's personality, who is at fault, and how the situation is hopeless and cannot be changed. The primary idea concerning this technique is to move the relational members past their mythology, which is totally based on the past, to start the effort of give-and-take in the present reality. This effort usually requires the therapist to outline the expectations, needs, and wants of each person and then to move both of them to a more trustworthy position of taking responsibility for obligations. Although the process of prescribing this give-and-take is slow, the balancing of obligations and entitlements eventually results in trustworthiness, which spurs more giving.

Salvage, Restoration, and Blessing

The reality of relationships is that many will be highly destructive and dysfunctional. In facing that reality, people must deal with one of three choices: cutoff, which tends to seal in destructive entitlement; salvage, which essentially means recognizing the mechanisms and causes of past dysfunction so that one can avoid taking those same or similar destructive actions in current relationships; or, restoration, which is to go back to the very relationship that caused the damage to see if it can now be loving and trustworthy. All three of these choices carry intergenerational consequences. In essence, this technique deals with the essential elements of love and trust that people hope to pass along to succeeding generations. As such, we feel that the word *bless-ing* is appropriate. Individuals, at some point in their lives, will leave some type of legacy concerning love and trust to those with whom they were intimately involved. We will stress here that blessing can be given to future generations from any of the previous positions: cutoff, salvage, or restoration. Also, it is important to recognize that each situation will present different relational risks, so restoration is not necessarily better than salvage. Transformation of relationships with these techniques, however, is among the most powerful in contextual therapy.

Final Thoughts on the Four Dimensions

In many ways, contextual therapy is complex because it deals with a blending of the different dimensions of reality. To complicate this, we add a dimension that includes a relational reality that spreads into the past and into the future, involving numerous generations. We hope, however, that through these first chapters you will see how contextual therapy is actually meant to be simple. The four dimensions are a way to help us organize our thoughts about assessment, direction of therapy, possible interventions, and hopeful transformations. The fact that the psychotherapist must pay attention to the four dimensions is not as confusing as it may seem. In actuality, it gives the helper a guide to understand how and why certain things work in therapy and others do not.

The Techniques
of Contextual Therapy

CHAPTER 6

Slapping the Face and Violations Impacting Self

The integrative nature of the contextual therapy approach lends itself to a variety of techniques that can and should be used in a clinical setting. We have discussed a number of the primary issues and interventions in the objectifiable dimensions of facts and systemic interactions. It is important to realize that we do not simply give lip service to the impact a psychotherapist can have in working with individuals and families by interventions made in these two dimensions. For instance, many times we become advocates and organizers for patients to get appropriate health care (factual dimension) or point out communication patterns that make change difficult (systemic transaction dimension). In order to integrate the information from the four dimensions, we must make interventions from sources of all four perspectives. However, the interventions in the factual and systemic transaction dimensions are fairly well known and are discussed in other resources. It is our task here to discuss interventions in the individual psychology and relational ethics dimensions because they are less well known and because the contextual perspective is unique in some of the change strategies.

When an intervention is made with one particular dimension in mind, however, it works across the dimensions in effect. Therefore, we are very comfortable with all types of interventions. We are reminded of a story that Bill O'Hanlon, an excellent solution-focused therapist, told in one of his seminars. He was trying to illustrate how absurd and misguided some therapies, especially psychodynamic therapies, are in helping people change. The story goes that a man landed from an airplane trip in a major city and needed to secure transportation to his hotel. He asks for help from someone who looks knowledgeable. "I need to get to this particular hotel," he says. The person responds, "Okay, but first, tell me where you are from." Confused, the man says, "Well, I'm from California, but I'm not sure what that has to do with getting to my hotel." "Be patient," the person says, "Now, tell me about your family." The man becomes a bit agitated and says, "Look, all I want to know is how to get to my hotel. Can you help me?" The person responds, "Of course, I can help you, but transportation has risks and does not come easy. Are you aware of how angry and resistant you are becoming? Maybe we should look at this at a deeper level."

Of course, O'Hanlon's point is well taken. Many times, what people need and want are "directions to their hotels," and as contextual therapists, we do not hesitate to make behavioral and solution-focused interventions when appropriate. But we would also counter that many people come to us saying they want to know a way to get to their hotels and we give them straight answers. We respond to the traveler, "You could take a taxi." "Oh, I never feel comfortable with taxi drivers. They may rip me off!" says the traveler. "Well," we say, "I suppose that you could take the bus that runs every hour." The traveler shoots back quickly, "And ride with all those people? They are not my kind." Finally, we suggest, "I guess if you don't want to take a taxi or ride a bus, maybe you could walk." The traveler becomes indignant, saying, "I came to you for help and the best you can do is suggest walking. I can't make it that far." At this point, if we are wise psychotherapists, we will say, "Okay, tell me where you are from."

The fact is that many patients who come under our care have sought change in a variety of ways. Some know very well about things they could do in the factual or systemic interaction dimensions that would make a significant difference in their lives. Still, however, they have internal emotional issues that either prevent them from taking the action or complicate their effectiveness in making changes. Most of the time, people have difficulty executing changes that they know they should make, they often have complicating factors in the dimensions of individual psychology or relational ethics.

Throughout the first section of this book, we have emphasized the essential elements of love and trust. These are not only the foundation of developing a healthy self-concept and self-esteem but are also the essential elements that form a healthy relational ethic to pass along to others. For example, in figure 6.1 we have illustrated that love and trust serve as foundational pillars to support the healthy development of an individual's personality and psychology. The individual, on the strength of his or her formation around love and trust, provides the foundation for the love and trust pillars that will support the family relational ethic. This relational ethic, in turn, is what en-

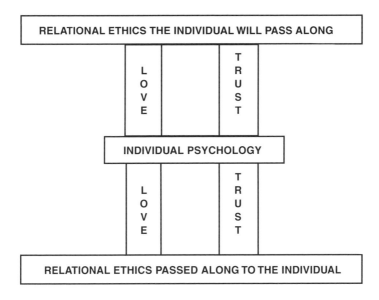

FIGURE 6.1. Illustration of How Love and Trust Support Subjective Dimensions

ables the next generation of individuals to feel love and to know that the family is trustworthy. Love and trust, then, more than any other factors, will determine the outcome of individual psychology and the strength and health of the relational ethics. Both of these dimensions rely on love and trust.

In this chapter, we will discuss interventions that can be used when there has been an insult or a violation of love and trust that impacts the individual's formation of self. In the next chapter, we will discuss transformational change strategies that primarily address violations of love and trust in the dimension of relational ethics. It is worth stating again, however, that changes initiated in one dimension will affect all other dimensions.

INTERVENTIONS WITH VIOLATIONS TO THE SENSE OF SELF

It is sometimes shocking for us to hear stories of the violations that individuals endure from their families. Murder, rape, incest, suicide, and abuse are just a few of the heinous acts that we hear about in our work. Because, however, the heart of the damage to the sense of self in the dimension of individual psychology consists of violations of love and trust, the damage need not be dramatic. Any time there is a question concerning love and trust, there is damage perpetuated to the individual. In order to illustrate the various techniques used in this dimension, we will focus on one particular case of a 37-year-old woman who sought therapy because she was continuing to have angry outbursts toward her husband and her children that included verbally attacking the children and, at times, physically attacking her husband. She had received an ultimatum from her husband to seek therapy and get "fixed" or leave the marriage. In the first session, the woman revealed the depth of the damage to her sense of self.

Woman: I know that it's me and my husband is right. He's basically a good guy, but he can do just the slightest little thing and I go ballistic. The same is true with my two boys.

Therapist: I'm not sure that it is all you. You have already told me about serious damage that you experienced in your family.

Woman: I know, but I don't want to use that as an excuse. I know it's me who is crazy.

Therapist: I don't really believe you are crazy. Often, I see people who have been seriously hurt in the past play out some of those things in the present. It isn't an excuse. It's just part of the reality that makes up who they are. You grew up in a place that was not safe and with a family that I am not sure loved you.

Woman: (Long pause) I have never known what to do with the past. This is difficult, but the thing that hurt me most was not being sexually abused by my father. It was the fact that my mother didn't believe me when I told her.

Therapist: (Long pause) What was it that your mother did when you told her?

Woman: When I told her what my father had been doing to me, she just stared at me with those angry eyes. It seemed like an eternity, but I was expecting her to go after Dad. Instead, she suddenly slapped me across the face and called me a slut.

Therapist: (Long pause) And how did you survive?

Woman: My father stopped abusing me then, but both of them just withdrew. We never said a word about it again, but I know that both of them blame me and hate me.

Therapist: Do you believe they still hate you?

Woman: I know they do. Last year when I was feeling really depressed, I stopped by to see my mother. I was really upset and crying and finally blurted out that I just wanted one person to love me. I looked her straight in the eye and told her I never knew if she loved me. You know what she did? She stared at me exactly like she did when I told her what my father had done to me. It was like I was being slapped in the face all over again.

The depth of this woman's pain was obvious. She had grown up in a household that offered no safety or solace. The father had violated trust with the daughter by sexually abusing her to meet his needs, instead of looking out for his daughter's interest. The mother further violated this trust by refusing to believe or protect the daughter. Although it was not clear from this interchange, it became clear in therapy that she had developed a way of dealing with these untrustworthy situations. She became hypervigilent concerning every family member's actions, so as to anticipate and protect herself from harm. In her relationships outside the family, she was very structured about what was acceptable and unacceptable to her and only participated in relationships if things were done her way. In short, she coped with the violations of trust in her family by becoming *controlling,* which is a power, or fight, response. But even more damaging than these obvious violations of trust was the fact that the woman had what she considered overt evidence that her parents did not love her. The attacks and the withdrawal from the parents left this woman with the harmful conclusion that there was something unlovable about her. This was clearly seen in her shaming, self-condemning behavior. Yet part of this woman also felt that her parents were dreadfully wrong in what they did to her. Her angry, attacking behavior with her own family indicated that not only did she cope with the lack of love by shaming herself, she coped by moving into raging outbursts. She had to answer the question of why she was not loved. Her answer, sometimes out of a fear response and sometimes out of a fight response, was to oscillate between believing that she was unlovable (shame) and believing that her parents were some kind of monsters who deserved punishment (rage). This woman had a highly disturbed sense of self, and it was playing out in the ways that she behaved with her family. The primary requirement of therapy, therefore, was to assist her in reorganizing her constructions around love and trustworthiness and thereby helping her rectify her seemingly uncontrollable and irrational behavior toward her own family.

Multidirected Partiality

Multidirected partiality is identified as the most important therapeutic tool for the contextual therapist (Boszormenyi-Nagy & Krasner, 1986). It is not only a therapeutic methodology or an intervention strategy; it is an attitude that a contextual therapist carries. In terms of attitude, multidirected partiality means that the psychotherapist is aware and accountable to all people in the relationships who may be potentially affected by interventions. It also assumes that all individuals who are concerned with difficult relationships are human beings and are equally entitled to the psychotherapist's consideration and respect of their humanity, as well as recognition of their side of the story in the intergenerational relational ledger (Boszormenyi-Nagy & Krasner, 1986). As a methodology, multidirected partiality is a technique of understanding and crediting all relational parties for the different concerns, efforts, and impacts of what people have done in relationships and what has been done to them. It is important to note that multidirected partiality is sequential siding with and recognition of the story of each family member and is not neutrality or impartiality (Goldenthal, 1996). There are specific aspects of the multidirected partiality technique. These are empathy, crediting, acknowledgment of efforts, and accountability (Goldenthal, 1996).

Empathy. It is an extremely well-recognized proposition that one of the most powerful healing and connecting aspects of the therapeutic relationship between psychotherapist and patient is empathy. The ability of the psychotherapist to make and to express emotional connections with a patient's loss, fear, pain, or difficulty cannot be overstated (Goldenthal, 1996). This aspect of multidirected partiality is the primary focal point of the psychotherapist being able to join with the patient (Hargrave & Anderson, 1992).

Crediting. There are actually two aspects of crediting. The first deals with the psychotherapist acknowledging and accepting the unfairness, violations, and relational insults that the patient has experienced in life (Goldenthal, 1996). If the patient feels that the psychotherapist has acknowledged his or her issues of relational violation, then the second aspect of crediting becomes possible. This is to credit the aspects of the relationship that were loving and trustworthy, apart from the harm that was perpetuated (Hargrave, 1994).

Acknowledgment of Efforts. The technique of acknowledgment of effort is related to crediting but changes focus. Instead of crediting the patient's relational issues of unfairness and violation, it focuses on the efforts and contributions that the patient has made to relationships. In showing partiality in this way, the psychotherapist usually acknowledges the patient's contributions first and then moves other people in the relationships to recognize the efforts of the patient (Goldenthal, 1996).

Accountability. Multidirected partiality does not only mean empathizing with and acknowledgment of the pain or violations caused by others. It moves past acknowledging a patient's contributions. It also includes holding the patient, as well as other relational parties, responsible for the actions and intended behaviors that have caused damage or will be violations of love and trustworthiness (Goldenthal, 1996).

In the previously mentioned case, the woman's beliefs about herself would hinder any type of effective therapy. Multidirected partiality is an excellent methodology for making a connection with the patient, forming a trustworthy bond between patient and psychotherapist, and then proceeding to set the stage for change and reorganization in the restructuring of cognitive constructions around self-image and behavior. In the following exchange, the therapist sought to establish an empathetic bond with the patient in order to join but also to clear confusion.

Therapist: Sometimes when there are so many confusing emotions that go on inside of you, it's hard to know whether they are emotions that belong to the past or the present.

Woman: What do you mean?

Therapist: You have had to carry around so much hurt, anger, and confusion from your relationship with your parents, it seems like those emotions come up in every relationship.

Woman: They do. I constantly feel like I am sad, mad, or hurt with everyone. I just think it's the way I am.

Therapist: Yes, I do believe that this is part of the way you are, but most people who have been abused feel all these emotions at the same time. They don't know how to sort emotions out, and this makes it hard to know how to relate to people.

Woman: Now, that's right on the money with me. I feel so many things at once that it's hard to know anything that I'm feeling.

Therapist: I understand this completely. When you come from an abusive background, the two most important things that you can get from family are thrown into question. You can't know if you are loved, and you can't know if you can trust the people around you to be safe.

Woman: I know that's true in my family.

Therapist: If I were in a place where I didn't think I was loved and didn't know if I could trust people, I would be afraid, angry, protective, controlling. I'd feel like there was something wrong with me or feel that there was always something wrong with the people who should have loved me.

Woman: I feel all of those things.

Therapist: I know. What I want you to also know is that I can understand how you came to those reactions. It's not because you are crazy. You are trying to deal with this overall collision of emotions. You probably have been dealing with it for years and years. It comes out in angry explosions sometimes; it comes out in depression; it comes out in being fearful.

Woman: You seem to understand this pretty well.

Therapist: I can't understand all of what you have felt, but I know what emotions are like. I believe that if I can help you sort out the emotions, we can begin to understand them separately and what each one is trying to tell you. If you can recognize emotions separately, they won't come all at once and feel like a tangled mess that ties you in such knots that you don't know what to do.

Woman: That would be so nice.

Here, the psychotherapist made a connection with the woman through understanding and articulating the emotions she felt. He expressed empathy by saying that he would feel similar things if he had been in the same situation, and he thereby suggested that other people would have felt similarly. Finally, he gave her hope by making sense of the confusion. He told her that she was not crazy, that the emotions came all at one time, and that therapy could help her separate the emotions. This hopefulness and understanding bonded the woman to the psychotherapist in a trustworthy interaction. Later in the same session, the psychotherapist worked to credit the woman's experience of violations.

Therapist: You have children. What is it that you believe your children deserve from you?

Woman: They deserve a mother who loves them and is always there for them. (Starts to weep.) They deserve a mother who won't fly into these angry rages.

Therapist: So, they deserve a mother who loves them and treats them correctly.

Woman: Yes.

Therapist: What do you think the effect will be if they do not get those two essential things from you?

Woman: I worry about that all the time. I am afraid that they won't feel confident about themselves and will make some of the same mistakes that I have.

Therapist: So, some of the actions that they miss from you would be your fault in their future relationships.

Woman: I feel that way.

Therapist: Then I suppose that it would be fair that the violations you experienced as a child affect the way you currently relate to your husband and children.

Woman: (Long pause) I don't want to use that as an excuse.

Therapist: I have no desire for you to use it as an excuse. I only have a desire for you to understand where these emotions came from.

Woman: Yes, it affects me.

Therapist: Yes. You deserved to be taught by your mother and father that you were unique and very special. You deserved to be taught that you were precious and something to always hold near and dear. You deserved to be taught that you were worthy and valuable enough for them to sacrifice their own good for you. You deserved to observe them treating you in a way that showed you that you were safe and protected from exploitation. Instead, you were told that you were dirty. There were many instances where they put their interests ahead of yours. And worse of all, they used you for sex and then blamed you for the consequences.

Woman: (Crying very hard) Why did they do those things?

Therapist: I'm not saying that they are bad people. I'm saying that when you deserved to be loved and to know that you

> could trust them, you were left to wonder what was wrong with you and to fend for yourself.

Woman: (Continuing to cry) So this happened to me. What do I do with it?

Therapist: We want to do many things with it, but for now, I want you to know that your behavior comes directly from those questions about who you are and how you are going to take care of yourself. Your parents are not evil, but they have inflicted you with a severe hurt that has never really been treated. We have to first recognize that there is a wound.

Woman: I hear so often from my husband that I'm crazy. It's really different to hear that I'm not. That there is a reason for all this.

Therapist: I know that there is a reason.

Woman: You know, my parents did some things right. I never went without anything and they always supported me in my athletics.

Therapist: Of course, they did some things right. They are not bad people. But you have a wound here that was inflicted by them. That wound is that they did not love you and act in a trustworthy way that you deserved.

The psychotherapist worked with the woman to recognize that she would hold herself responsible for having an effect on her children, so she must do the same with regard to her own parents. By setting this foundation, the psychotherapist was able to then articulate what exactly the woman deserved and what she was denied. This crediting further bonded the woman with the psychotherapist in trust and allowed her to legitimately look at the wound that was caused by the violations. In the next session, the psychotherapist expanded the multidirected partiality to acknowledge her efforts in the families.

Woman: Last week was very important to me. I felt like for the first time I could finally look at the hole in me that I always felt.

Therapist: What did you find in the hole?

Woman: I just felt that I could finally say that there was something really wrong with the way I grew up. We looked okay on the outside; it was never okay for me to look at what was wrong.

Therapist: And what did you discover was wrong?

Woman: I never knew for sure that they loved me. At times they would care for me, and it felt good. But I always have felt that they looked at me differently. And, of course, I was totally violated by my dad. He could go to prison today for what he did to me.

Therapist: He still could.

Woman: I don't want to go there.

Therapist: That's fine. I just wanted you to know that you had the power to take action. What he did was clearly wrong and your mother's response was clearly wrong.

Woman: Yes. That's what makes me feel good. Finally being able to say it out loud.

Therapist: Good. Let's go a little further then. Facing those two realities of having to guess if there was love for you and knowing that they would exploit you, how did you learn to cope?

Woman: I don't know. I just muddled along.

Therapist: That is a way to cope. But you also found other ways. When you don't know if your husband loves you—when he is mad at you or threatening to leave—what do you do?

Woman: (Thinks for a moment.) I feel awful. I think that he is right sometimes. But sometimes, I will take him on and just shove it right back in his face.

Therapist: That is what I suspect you did with your parents. When you were not sure, you probably became very sad and may have thought that they were right. That there was something wrong with you and that you were unlovable. You probably got a little depressed and then tried to do things that would make them love you. Does any of that fit?

Woman: That's exactly what I did. I was always trying to get them to recognize me. I did that especially in athletics.

Therapist: Other times, you might have thought something like, "The hell with them. I don't care what they think."

Woman: I would. Even though I would try and please them, if I was angry, I would take either or both of them on. Especially as I got older, I just wouldn't let them get to me.

Therapist:	These two things. Getting depressed and working hard to please when you felt shameful and getting angry when you had enough—these were your ways of coping. It's how you muddled through. Without those two things—which are big sacrifices on your part—you might have gone crazy for real.
Woman:	I never thought of it that way. Are you saying that my depression and anger are good things?
Therapist:	Not good in the sense that they have desirable results, but good in the sense that you found a way to stay connected with your parents, stay on course and excel in athletics, and grow to adulthood. When you think about how severe a wound you had, it's amazing that you have coped as well as you have.
Woman:	That's the first time that anyone has ever said that I cope. They usually say I can't deal with anything.

The psychotherapist acknowledged the woman's efforts by pointing out that the very behavior that was dysfunctional was a way for her to cope and stay in her family. Later in the session, the psychotherapist made the same therapeutic move by tying her controlling behavior as a coping skill to the violations of trustworthiness that the woman suffered. As a result, the woman began to feel cognitively that there were legitimate reasons for her actions and began to move toward restructuring her belief system about herself. The psychotherapist shifted the therapy to another therapeutic technique but used multidirected partiality in the later sessions to call in accountability.

It is worth restating here that multidirected partiality is not only a methodology but a therapeutic attitude. Three sessions into the therapy, the psychotherapist is primarily partial to the woman's plight but alludes to understanding her parents. He will be partial to the parents and to the woman's husband and the children's issues as the therapy proceeds. However, the partiality shown here in these initial sessions has created a trustworthy bond between psychotherapist and patient, as well as formed the perspective in the woman that there are different possibilities for her self-image and behavior.

Understanding

Understanding is a therapeutic technique outlined by Hargrave (1994, 2001) that helps individuals who have suffered violations of love and trust to come to different conclusions about themselves and about the people who perpetrated the violations. Although "understanding" carries the therapeutic attitude of multidirected partiality, we outline it here as a separate contextual therapeutic technique because it offers more specificity. When people experience questions regarding violations by the people who should have loved them, they naturally turn to the question "Why was I not loved?" This question is a fundamental response to the construction of an individual's psychology, found in dimension two. When there is love, people will regard themselves as unique, precious, and worthy. But when there is a question of love, then the question becomes a driving force to find a way to cope with this disturbing truth (Hargrave, 1994).

As discussed earlier in chapter 3, individuals typically answer this question of "Why was I not loved?" in extremes. One extreme is to hold the person who should have given love as culpable for the violation. This culpability is not wrong, in and of itself. Indeed, the person who should have given love and did not is irresponsible and culpable. However, in dealing with the culpability, the damaged party begins to hold the person responsible not only for the violation but also for how the violation *made him or her feel*. When an essential family member does not love us or, at the minimum, express love to us, we feel unwanted, unworthy, and undeserving. How could this family member do such a thing to us? This can easily turn into indignation and move quickly to extreme anger or rage. The unfortunate thing about rage is that it separates us from the humanity of the people who damaged us. No longer are they people, like us, who made unfortunate choices and mistakes; they are evil monsters who did nothing but cause harm (Hargrave, 1994).

Contextually, this sets the stage for relationships that have to be dysfunctional. If the victimizer is a monster who is beyond reason or goodness, then we must say that the victimizer is doing what he or she is built to do. That is, be a monster. As victims, we are tied to the monster because of our family relation, and we want that relationship to provide us with love. But, of course, no monster who is evil can provide such love. In this situation, there is no love that the victim can receive and no responsibility for which the monster can be held accountable (Hargrave, 1994).

Of course, people are not monsters. All people have circumstances and realities that shape behavior. All people are human. Humans, however, are responsible for their actions. In order to hold people responsible for their actions, the person who did not receive love cannot lose touch with the victimizer's humanity by spinning into an emotional rage. He or she must hold the person who was irresponsible accountable for the action. This can only be done successfully by understanding the circumstances, limitations, development, and efforts of the person who caused the violation (Hargrave, 1994).

Rage is not the only extreme response that can come from the question. Another result is for people who experienced the violation to believe that they are unlovable. Essentially, people internalize the belief that these family members were correct in rejecting them because they are defective. In these instances, the individuals develop a core construct of shame. People who take this direction feel as if they deserve nothing, they are never right, and they can never be accepted for who they are. They may turn to depression over the heavy burden, secrecy to cover from others the unacceptableness of their being, or performance or achievement as a means to gather affirmation from others. But although rage leads us to lose touch with the humanity of the person who violated us, shame leads us to lose touch with our own humanity. Shame has devastating consequences (Hargrave, 2001).

The technique of understanding is essentially about *helping the person who experienced the violation to understand and recognize the limitations, circumstances, and development of the person who perpetuated the damage and to realize that in the same position, he or she might have made similar mistakes*. Essentially, it is about the person who experienced the violation putting himself or herself in the shoes of the one who performed the violation. This has two effects. First, understanding has the power to alleviate pain and to make a new cognitive construction of self possible. No longer do family members have to be monsters or do victims have to be unworthy beings. It becomes clear that most people are simply flawed and make unfortunate mistakes in the efforts of loving and being trustworthy. Second, it sets the foundation for the person who has experienced the violation to take responsibility for his or her actions that may violate love and trust (Hargrave, 2001).

In the case of this woman, she experienced a common cyclical response of alternating shame and rage responses. In the fourth session, the psychotherapist moved her to the point of confronting some of the past events involving her parents, in order to give her relief from her pain and also to make a new construction of self possible.

Therapist: Tell me a bit about your parents and the families that they grew up in.

Woman: My mother was the eldest in her family. My grandfather was really distant from the family, and I believe that my grandmother wore the pants in the family.

Therapist: What was your mother's place?

Woman: She always said that she raised her two younger sisters and brother. She told me that she never could remember a time when she wasn't responsible for taking care of a child.

Therapist: And your father?

Woman: Irish/Catholic. A lot of alcoholism and chaos. My father was the middle of six. I never had much to do with my grandparents on my father's side. In fact, I only saw them alive one time, at my dad's older brother's funeral.

Therapist: And how did your mother and father meet?

Woman: They met when my father was on leave from Korea. They were from the same town but a few years apart in age. When my father was on leave, they met at a dance or something.

Therapist: How do you think their family experiences were?

Woman: I really don't know much. They never talked about it.

Therapist: Is there someone safe on either side of the family whom you could ask?

The woman identified an aunt on her mother's side whom she was close to. The psychotherapist sent the woman home to speak with this aunt, to find out about her mother's experiences in the family. She returned the next session with surprising information.

Woman: I spoke with my aunt and she gave me an earful. She told me that my grandfather was a quiet man but certainly not timid. She said that he had several affairs during the time that they were young and virtually hated my grandmother. She said that grandmother knew about the affairs but essentially just ignored him because she didn't like him either. She said it was like an ice house. Evidently, my grandmother made my mom her partner and leaned on her like she should have leaned on a husband. My aunt says that my mother was very much like her mom, but that she was always looking for a way out. She told me that she wasn't really ever sure if my mother was in love with my dad, or if it was just a way to get away.

Therapist: It sounds pretty overbearing.

Woman: This is the juiciest piece. My aunt does not have any idea
            of what happened to me—the sexual abuse from my fa-
            ther. He had hit on her! He tried to make a move on his
            wife's sister.

Therapist: How did she handle it?

Woman: She said that she got right up in his face and told him that
            if he ever made another move toward her, she would go
            straight to her sister.

There was obviously a situation where this woman's mother had
grown up in a parentified position, with a cold emotional atmosphere,
whereas her father was suspected of growing up in a highly chaotic
framework that produced sexually acting-out behavior. The psychotherapist used these revelations to make the understanding connection between this woman and her parents.

Therapist: Emotionally, what do you think it was like for your mother?

Woman: I thought about that. I think that she was overwhelmed by
            my grandmother. She probably was the one who heard all
            her mother's complaints about her father. I was thinking
            that she thinks that men are never to be trusted. At least,
            that's what I would think.

Therapist: How else do you think she responded?

Woman: I think that's why she is so controlling. She manages ev-
            erything. That's the way her mother did it, so that's the
            way she did it. If men can't be depended on, you have to
            do it yourself.

Therapist: You have said that you are also controlling.

Woman: Yeah. I think I do it because I have to know everything is
            settled.

Therapist: Is there a chance that your mother also does that?

Woman: I would imagine that's at least part of it.

Therapist: Now a hard question. This woman who is your mother,
            who grew up in this environment where her father was
            not trustworthy. Who grew up with a controlling mother
            who coopted her into co-managing the family. Who grew
            up in an emotionally cold environment. Who married a
            man whom she may or may not have loved. Who may not
            trust men. Who likely chooses to manage all this by keep-
            ing everything settled. Why do you think this woman

slapped you in the face when you told her what your father was doing to you?

Woman: (Thinks for a long time.) I think she was doing the same thing that I do. When something gets in the way and causes upset, you get rid of it, ignore it, or make it behave. (Long pause) I think that I was upsetting my mother's life and she was making me behave so everything could be okay.

Therapist: And after you did, she ignored it.

Woman: Yeah. Both of them did.

Therapist: (Long pause) Does that make any sense to you?

Woman: It makes sense, in that my mother was doing what she had to do to keep her life controlled.

Therapist: It was a bad choice to sacrifice you to keep her life in control.

Woman: Yes, but I know I do some of the same things with my family. I'm not consciously thinking all the time that I'm sacrificing them so I'll be okay. I just do it.

Therapist: So your mother might have just done it.

Woman: Yes.

Therapist: If that's true, it would mean that your mother doesn't hate you any more than you hate your children. She just can't handle it when things get ugly.

Woman: I think that's right.

As the session went on, the therapist also made connections with the father's behaviors, although information on his background was much more sketchy. But as the woman related to the past of her mother and made identification with it, she became more confident. Her mother no longer seemed a threat to her but instead became a woman who struggled with pain just as she had. Instead of her mother being a source of pain, the woman became secure enough to consider other possibilities for the reason her mother was rejecting and abusive when her daughter experienced her time of greatest need. During the week after the session and without the psychotherapist's direction, the woman took her mother out to lunch, asked her specific questions about her family, and confirmed many of the feelings that were identified in the session. At the end, the woman told her mother that many things were also hard in her growing-up years and that she has been left with some of the same feelings as her mother's. She reported during the next session, "My mother shot that glance back at me—you know the one that I told you about before. She knew exactly what I was talking about and was telling me not to go there. But you know, it didn't feel the same to me. I think I was sitting there with the same look on my face. I was thinking that I'm not ever going to let your need for everything to be okay make me think that there is something wrong with me." The woman clearly was identifying strength and a clear reconstruction of her sense of self. Instead of blaming herself, she knew that her mother had strange coping skills. Also interesting was the fact that the woman did not have real anger toward her mother. She identified that she could not be angry at her mother too much because she might have done the same thing. "I'm not angry at her. I feel sorry for her. She is going to continue to carry this stuff around with her. I'm getting better," she said.

Teaching Self-Care

One of the elements that becomes essential when people have a damaged sense of self because of love and trust violations is to create the opportunity for them to reshape behaviors and beliefs. As mentioned before, the psychotherapist is not strong enough or important enough to pronounce a person loved and to reshape trustworthiness. This reshaping must come from one of three places: (1) redress from the people who should have loved and been trustworthy in the first place; (2) the person reshaping his or her own beliefs and actions; or (3) the person using spiritual resources, if appropriate.

Redress From Others. As contextual therapists, we always see positive possibilities for even the most damaging of families. This does not mean that all violations of love and trust can be addressed. Sometimes the people who caused the damage are still just as damaging now as in the past. In other cases, the people who violated love and trust that resulted in the perturbed sense of self are no longer available or are dead. Wherever possible, however, we have found that when the people who are responsible for the violation can speak directly about love and trust in a different way than they did when they caused damage, it can have dramatic results. It is like putting a new hard drive, or at least a new program, in an older computer. Family members retain power to speak to our needs for love and security like no other people can. Therefore, it is a worthy effort to have this redress, if possible (Hargrave, 2001).

Several factors make this a possibility. First, many people become wiser as they mature. They see, many years after the fact, that they did not provide the strong sense of love that the relationships in their charge deserved or that they were not responsible and reliable in providing care. As people grow older, many will see these mistakes and be willing to be loving and trustworthy in the present. In these cases, mostly what is needed is specificity and opportunity. The psychotherapist can help with specificity by facilitating communication and by articulating specifically what is needed in terms of communicating love and trust. Essentially, the psychotherapist provides a map for people to follow. In the same fashion, the psychotherapist can suggest or supply the opportunities for loving and trustworthy interchanges, both in and out of therapy.

Second, redress is possible because the therapist can help people to understand the intergenerational framework that has shaped the revolving slate of injustices that exists in the family. It seldom happens that when damaging individuals have their issues of the past recognized and credited that they do not recognize and credit the issues and the past that they have created with another. The contextual therapist knows that most times, victimizers were once victims themselves. If this information is accessed and credited, the possibility is great that a person who once denied love and trust will be able to supply it.

Finally, people prefer reconciliation and good relationships over bad ones. Despite the popular notion of the satisfaction of revenge that is often found in media, most people prefer to be at peace with and close to their families. Most desire resolution because they know that reconciliation and providing love and trust are ultimately the only ways that families survive (Hargrave, 1994).

In the case of this woman, redress was still a risky proposition. The mother and the father were still very distant and defensive at this point in the therapy. The mother's hesitancy at her daughter's statement was an indication. Also, enormous issues remained with the father's sexual abuse. However, 4 years after this therapy ended, the woman did come back to therapy to work on communicating with her parents. Although her mother was still quite cold, emotionally, the woman and her father made progress because the father took responsibility for the sexual abuse he perpetrated.

Reshaping Beliefs. One of the amazing powers of humans is to understand and choose cognitive reconstruction. We believe, from a contextual perspective, that once individuals understand the basic needs for their sense of self and a basis for trustworthiness, they can weed out faulty constructions that were a result of a family member's abuse, neglect, and irresponsibility and can construct new ones that are healthy and helpful. Even though this is done on an individual cognitive level, it is facilitated most often by relationships. For instance, many of our patients have benefited from group therapy where the focus is on confronting old ideas about the self and encouraging present responsibility to obligations. Likewise, other patients benefit from reading self-help books or books about the experiences of others. These "how to" resources show and model how people go about finding new definitions of themselves. Finally, it is helpful to process information and ideas about love and trust with family members who were not directly responsible for the violations of love and trust. Most often, these other family members are siblings, but they may also be extended family, such as was the case with this woman's aunt.

The key in reshaping these beliefs is for patients to be aware of what they are trying to do and to make use of new information that comes from books, family members, or group therapy. The woman in the case example not only made good use of processing with other family members (first her aunt and later one of her siblings), but she also was helped significantly by reading books about sexual abuse.

Spiritual Resources. Not every patient has spiritual beliefs, but many do. We concur with Doherty (1996) that the tendency of psychotherapy to be morally neutral or to avoid spiritual issues is a mistake. First, we are not morally neutral, and it is impossible to do therapy without taking some positions. Second, spirituality is an obvious resource to many patients and should be used as a strength whenever possible.

The psychotherapist does not have to become an expert in all spiritual resources and religions; however, it is essential for the psychotherapist to treat spirituality as a multicultural or a gender issue of which to become more aware of and to use where appropriate. Most spiritual resources, at their foundation, promote a sense of love, peace, honor, tranquillity, trustworthiness, and community. In many cases, people can gain a feeling that God loves them and is trustworthy or that some type of community loves them and is trustworthy. In both cases, the contextual therapist should be open to encouraging and exploring these resources with the patient to help reshape the issues of love and trust.

Practicing New Behaviors in the Old Landscape

Another powerful technique in assisting patients to address violations that have impacted their sense of self is to help them pattern new behaviors to confirm new cognitive constructions. Part of the difficulty with the woman in this case was that for years she carried the idea that she was unlovable, that there was something wrong with her, and that she had to keep control of everything to make sure she would not be hurt. She patterned a behavior in her family that directly fit with those beliefs. For instance, she tried to be a "supermom" by working and caring for her children. When, however, she experienced normal everyday failures, such as not having dinner cooked or being late to an appointment, she either went into self-condemning behavior about her "inadequacies as a person" or became angry because she "never received enough help." When one of her children or her husband tried to take responsibility for a duty, she likewise felt inadequate because she could not "handle the job herself," or she demanded that the child or her husband do the job exactly as she would do it, in order to maintain control. Another issue is that it was very important to her that her husband be well liked by others. However, any time he spent time at parties or activities talking to others and did not directly include her, she became jealous and raged at his behavior. After the rage, she condemned herself by saying that she was an "out of control fool" and didn't deserve her husband wanting to be around her. Although these behaviors fit well with her current beliefs about herself and her actions, they were the very behaviors that resulted in the instability of her marriage. The goal of practicing new behaviors in the old landscape is to confirm the new constructions of love and trust in the environment.

In looking at these behaviors, we feel that the overwhelming majority comes from the very basic emotional violations. In other words, there are not dozens of reasons that patients perform unreasonable or dysfunctional actions; there are a few basic issues. This construction by the therapist can be very helpful for patients, in that they learn not to work on every behavior they manifest, but instead learn how to focus on emotions they experience. For instance, this woman felt specific emotions associated with rage, shame, and control. The psychotherapist was then able to focus on these specific emotions and help her to make alternate behavior choices instead of falling into the old patterns of behavior that she usually did with her family. In short, the psychotherapist helps to create new behavior patterns in the old environmental landscape.

The patient usually does not make these changes all at once. Rather, it takes much practice and recognition through several sessions (Hargrave, 2000). As patients learn these new behaviors, however, the process also teaches them to be accountable and responsible for actions in relationships. As patients are responsible and trustworthy, their behavior confirms the new construction of self that they are now lovable and trustworthy in current relationships (Goldenthal, 1996).

Beginning in the sixth session, the psychotherapist started to direct the woman to recognize emotions and practice new behaviors.

Therapist: I notice that you have made tremendous progress in seeing how your past relates to your current behavior. You
have done an excellent job at confronting the ideas that
you developed from your childhood. I think that it's now
time to take it a step further.

Woman: I'm ready to do whatever. I just know that this is working.

Therapist: The situation that you originally came in for was the sud-
den outbursts of anger that you had with your husband
and children. I know that you have already felt some relief
in the way that you relate to them, but I feel that you are
now ready to take full responsibility for not going back to
those harmful tendencies.

Woman: I know that I'm not perfect at this. I'm better, but I still feel
like I'm holding back. I haven't done very well at all in not
demanding that things be done my way.

Therapist: I want you to think about three different situations in the
last year when you had these emotions. Rage at others.
Ashamed of yourself. Out of control of a situation.

Woman: (Thinks for a moment.) The rage is easy. My husband was
in the kitchen, talking to his dad and brothers last Thanks-
giving and leaving me to visit with his mother and sisters.
I have told him that I don't like to be with them and they
drive me nuts. I was stuck, and he was in there laughing
and having a good time. I lost it and went into the kitchen
and started yelling at him in front of his whole family.

Ashamed. I guess right after we got into the car to go
home. That's when he told me that I had to get help or he
was leaving. He said I could yell at him all I wanted, but
when I did it in public or in front of his family, I had gone
too far. I knew he was right and felt so bad.

(Pause) This may not be a very good example, but it's
the only one I can think of recently. My son was playing
baseball with his team. The field was muddy because of
all the rain, and the boys were just getting muddier and
muddier. I know it sounds crazy, but I just couldn't sit still.

I wanted to do something because those boys were getting so filthy. I was so uptight because all I could think about was how to wash my son's uniform.

Therapist: Those are good examples. Now, take each one. Just before you took the action, what was the message that went through your head?

Woman: (Thinks a very long time.) This is hard. With the rage, it was "I don't have to put up with this anymore." With being ashamed, it was "He is right. I am such a bitch." I guess with the uniforms it was "I've got to do something."

Therapist: Very good. What I want to tell you is that I believe that around 90% of the behavior that you have that causes you problems in your family are related to those three messages. I don't have to put up with this anymore. They are right, I'm so awful. And I have to do something. Those three messages relate directly back to what you received in your family. You knew at a deep level that your parents weren't doing you right. Especially as an adolescent. You would go into a rage because you didn't have to put up with it. You feared that your parents were right in not loving you. You were so awful. And when things got out of your control because you learned that life can really hurt you, you had to do something.

Woman: There is little doubt about that.

Therapist: Every time you run across something that reminds you of someone not doing you right, you not being okay, or something being out of your control, you have an automatic circuit that kicks in one of those statements that you learned long ago. But now that you have been breaking up some of those wrong thoughts about yourself, we can now make an effort to do something else with the message.

Here, the psychotherapist helped to tie the construction of individual psychology to a simple way of recognizing when behaviors were about to become dysfunctional. This construction was simplified not because it is always simple, but because the woman, like many who experience violations, got lost when she felt a tangle of emotions. Limiting the issue to three root emotions helped her to take more responsibility.

Woman: How do I do that?

Therapist: First, instead of just kicking into automatic pilot, you must slow everything down. Especially when you are experiencing emotions. Second, I want you to learn to recognize the message that you are feeling.

Woman: I'm not sure I understand.

Therapist: Before you "just react" to anything, I want you to analyze it first. Ask yourself about "I don't have to put up with this." "They are right, I am awful." "I have to do something."

Woman: Okay, then what?

Therapist: Then, I want you to give yourself an answer to those issues and emotions. For instance, what is your answer, based on the new you, to "I have to do something."

Woman: No, you don't. (Laughs)

Therapist: Good. Why?

Woman: Because in actuality, it probably isn't that important. Now, I don't know if I can believe that when I'm at the baseball game, but it's what I think.

Therapist: Then maybe you should come up with one more addition. No, I don't. So I probably should put my mind on something else I could do.

Woman: Now, I could probably do that.

Therapist: In other words, you make a choice based on who you are now instead of on the automatic reaction of who you were.

The psychotherapist gave the woman specifics about how to counter the old messages by adding to the messages. Such constructions assist patients to integrate something new with something familiar. The therapist worked with the woman on similar constructions to address the statements she gave herself concerning the rage and the shame. Although she was far from perfect, she made noticeable progress and family members began to comment. In the eighth session, she commented on an interaction with her husband.

Woman: We were all going to the movie last Friday. My husband and kids went on into the theater while I stayed to get popcorn and drinks. In trying to get all the stuff back, I dropped the drink carrier. I was so frustrated, I grabbed the popcorn and stopped before going into the theater. Then it came across me. YOU DON'T HAVE TO PUT UP WITH THIS.

I swear. I stopped dead in my tracks and heard: NO, YOU DON'T. BUT YOU DON'T HAVE TO GET BALLISTIC. (Laughs) I took a few deep breaths and went and got my husband. I told him that I was just about to blow, but I decided instead that what I really needed was some help.

Therapist: What did he do?

Woman: He said that he was sorry and went back for the drinks himself.

Therapist: And how was that for you?

Woman: Oh, so much better. It finally hit me. I don't have to continue making the same mistakes. I really am changing.

Therapist: Did your husband say anything else to you?

Woman: Before I came over here today, he said that he could tell how hard I was trying and that he and the kids have noticed how I'm handling things differently.

Therapist: It's because you are different.

The woman continued therapy for a total of 15 sessions. The effort of practicing emotional recognition and choosing different behaviors was a "two steps forward, one step back" proposition, but she continued to shift more and more of her behavior to being constructive. Every time she accomplished a behavioral shift, it confirmed to her more and more that she was forming a new sense of self that was both loving and trustworthy. Most important, however, was the fact that she was integrating this new behavior, with the result of creating a new trustworthiness with her husband and children.

CHAPTER 7

Sinking Sand and Violations That Impact Relational Ethics

Love and trust are the foundational pillars on which individuals build their personality, sense of self, and emotional framework. But, as we have mentioned before, individuals then use these elements to interact in relationships in either a loving and trustworthy manner or in a way that will detract from the relational resources of the family. It is essential for the contextual therapist to remember that individuals both carry the effect of the past in the formation of their individual psychology and propagate the future with the way they act in a caring and balanced manner in other relationships. Because each generation of humans takes in more and more relationships, the potential relational ethic we pass on is enormous. For instance, in Terry Hargrave's family, a total of 4 children were produced by his parents. From those 4 children, 12 more sons and daughters were produced. Now, from those sons and daughters, 7 more children, and counting, have been born. In Franz Pfitzer's family, he is the eldest of 5 children. These 5 children produced 14 more children. In both intergenerational groups, the way we deal with love and trust in the family relationships forms an intergenerational link that is essential for the formation of other secure links in the future. Even if our lineage four generations from now knows nothing about us—not our lifestyles, personalities, or even names—the way that we lived out love and trust within the family will either strengthen or weaken the legacy our descendants live with in regard to love and trust.

It is, then, a long-lasting opportunity to take relationships and families whose lives are having a bad effect on the relational ledger and turn them toward making significant contributions. All psychotherapists, but especially those who call themselves contextual therapists, must have this as a guiding principle in their work. It is, however, delicate and hard work to get damaging relationships turned around. In essence, we, as psychotherapists, are being asked to take people who have received the ill effects of relational ethics from bad relationships and to help them make healing and healthy choices for future generations. We are called on to make abundant emotional resources out of individuals who have meager and insufficient resources. If this sounds a little like Jesus taking a few loaves and fishes to feed 5,000, that actually is a little like our task as psychotherapists. Although this is the challenge, the good news is that when people use their resources, even meager ones, in loving and trustworthy ways, more resources are produced. Our task in this final chapter, then, is to discuss the techniques that have a transformational potential to strengthen the family resources and to put relational ethics in better stead.

TRANSFORMATION OF FAMILY RESOURCES TOWARD STRENGTH

It is important to remind the reader that the attitude of the contextual therapist is one of multidirected partiality. The elements of empathy, crediting, acknowledgment, and accountability should always be present in the psychotherapist as he or she uses various techniques that effect change in the family. However, multidirected partiality needs more specificity in terms of technique to help psychotherapists understand the opportunities that exist for change. Although we want to make it clear that we do not reject multidirected partiality, we feel that in the dimension of relational ethics, it needs an enhancement of technique in order to help along change and to give family members a new direction regarding their legacy.

In the following case example, a highly complex and destructive family presented for therapy. The therapy began when a man in his mid-70s came in, depressed and contemplating suicide. He had been a successful home builder but now was in the position of declaring bankruptcy. His wife was ambivalent toward both his depression and the possibility of his suicide because she had been a victim of his neglect and verbal abuse for many of their 43 years of marriage. He had two sons and one daughter, all of whom were embittered toward the father for his critical and meddling ways in their lives. The eldest son had been in business with the father and now stood to lose his means of support. The second son had been married and divorced twice and had a successful accounting practice. The daughter had a history of drug abuse, had not married but had an adolescent son, and was going back to school to work on a degree in law enforcement. The man was very depressed as he expressed his feelings toward his life.

Man: All my life I've worked hard. I've made a business that has provided for us well. Just at the time in my life when I thought I would be taking it easy, the economy has gone south and I was left out to twist in the wind, with several houses unsold. Just when I really need my family, they all look at me and shrug their shoulders. They say, "What do you want from me?" They don't care at all. The more depressed I get, the more they feel like I deserve exactly what I am getting. It is a hell of a thing to live your whole life and get to the end and have nothing. No hope. No money. No family. It's like building a mansion on sand. It looks good for a while, but when the sand sinks, you can't salvage anything.

The man came to therapy alone for the first session, at the insistence of his family doctor. At the psychotherapist's request, he brought his wife with him for the second session. If there was any doubt with regard to the man's description of the rejection he felt, it was erased when the wife described her anger and resentment toward the husband.

Therapist: I appreciate your being willing to come in.

Woman: I don't know what I can do. We have all told him for years that he needed to get out and let Joe [the eldest son] run the business. He kept pushing to build more—this crazy idea that he wanted to build more houses in this city than another builder. Well, he's done it now. Now we only have our retirement to live on and he has left Joe in a terrible mess. He deserves what he's gotten, but it has taken the rest of us down with him. He has been awful to live with and the only thing that made it tolerable was that I had everything I wanted. Now that's gone. Frankly, if he doesn't feel so good, it's just fine with me. We haven't felt good for his whole life.

Therapist: And his talk of suicide?

Woman: I don't want him to kill himself. I think that would eventually make me feel bad. (Long pause) I don't know. I know

> there have been many times that I wished he were dead. I
> don't know what I feel. I know it wouldn't be good for
> him to kill himself.

Taking into account the first dimension of facts, there were serious physical and financial dynamics at work that complicated an already destructive family. The psychotherapist received a release to
speak with the son to find out what the father absolutely needed to
do with regard to the bankruptcy. After minimizing the workload on
the father, the psychotherapist consulted with a psychiatrist, and the
man started a regime of antidepressant medication. Although the father had made a contract with the psychotherapist not to harm himself, he was at great risk because of the level of damage and dysfunction
that had gone on in the family in the past and what was being perpetuated currently. During the third session, the psychotherapist started
working on transforming the damage that existed in the family.

Right Script but Wrong Players

As mentioned before, the key of this strategy is to help individuals
recognize that they have a legitimate relational claim, but that they
are trying to redeem or play out that claim with the wrong people.
The elements of this technique are to move individuals to the point
where they clearly recognize their relational claims, make overt the
inappropriateness of demanding the claim from other relationships,
and then help them get their entitlement addressed in a more appropriate fashion. In the previous two sessions the psychotherapist had
learned several things about the background of the man. He came
from a family of four, in which his father was an alcoholic who died
when he was 10 years old. His mother put pressure on him to help
her care for his younger siblings, but he would have none of it. By
the time he was 14, he had several run-ins with the law over delinquent behavior and finally left home. He had been on his own since
that time and worked at various construction jobs, eventually learning the trade of carpentry. While at these jobs, he consistently sent
money home to help his mother and his siblings, but he refused to
actually go home. He worked very hard and by the time he had met
and married his wife, he started building one house on his own, in
addition to keeping his carpentry job. From this beginning, he had
become a substantial home builder in the area.

Recognizing the Relational Claim. The psychotherapist became particularly interested in the man sending money home to take care of his mother and his siblings but refusing to go home. This behavior was certainly similar to the descriptions about him in his own family, of working all the time to provide money but not having any substantial kind of relationship with family members.

Therapist: Tell me. When you were younger, what was the mood of your family after your father died?

Man: Some of it was bad because we knew we were on our own. But he really wasn't good for much because he was a drunk. Sometimes he would give mother money for food, sometimes he would just drink it up.

Therapist: Are there any good memories of him?

Man: Not much. I didn't hate him. He was likable and easy to get along with. He wasn't a mean drunk.

Therapist: And how about your mother?

Man: Now there was a mean woman. I cannot remember a time when she wasn't on me about something. Constantly on me about doing this or that for her.

Therapist: I would imagine that if your father was unreliable, she saw you as the next logical person to count on.

Man: I think that was it. (Chuckles slightly.) Of course, she found out quickly that it wouldn't work.

Therapist: How so?

Man: I just knew that I didn't want to get swallowed up by her. I remember thinking, probably a week after my father died, that if I tried for 100 years, there was always going to be something else that my mother wanted from me. So I just refused to do any of it. I would go hang out somewhere and usually get into some trouble.

Therapist: How did you leave home?

Man: I had gotten in a fight at the pool hall and was hauled down to the police station. My mother came and got me. She had said this before, but she said, "You are going to turn out to be just like your father." But this time I said, "Maybe so, but I ain't going to turn out to be your husband." That was it. She told me never to come home. It was okay by me because I learned quickly to take care of myself.

Here the client described a situation where he had some loyalty
to his father because the man was his father and was likable but had
no obligation toward his father. He had an obligation toward his
mother, but he rejected the loyalty toward her and thereby rejected
the relationship. The psychotherapist wanted to help the man recognize that this situation presented a relational ledger issue that set a
tone for his fundamental life beliefs about work and relationships.

Therapist: It seems to me that there were two strange things that
were demonstrated in your family. Your father was irresponsible but was free; your mother was responsible but a
prison.

Man: You could put it that way.

Therapist: Which do you think you are?

Man: (Thinks for a moment.) I don't know. (Looking at his wife)
I guess you would say I'm irresponsible.

Woman: You are hard-working, but you haven't been much of a
husband or father.

Man: I always felt like I was responsible for everything. That's
why I worked so hard. I remember my mother's surprise
when I became a carpenter and was making good money
and started sending it home to her. She never once thanked
me for one dollar I sent.

Therapist: Did that bother you?

Man: Not really. I didn't really send it to get thanks. I sent it to
her because I wanted her to know how wrong she was
about me.

Therapist: (Long pause) I know this sounds a bit strange, but I would
at least like you to consider something for a minute. You
were deserving of a father to take care of you. You didn't
have one. Your mother shoved his responsibility to you.
You deserved a mother who would nurture you as you
learned to live your life. You got one who demanded that
you live life for her. So it seems to me that you were
cheated out of a couple of things when you were young.

Man: What was that?

Therapist: You were cheated out of care and freedom to be yourself.
I think I know what you did in response to your freedom,
I don't know what you did about the care.

Woman: He has always done what he has damned well pleased.

Therapist: I'm sure that it appears that way. (Looking at the man.) But I know that you work so hard because you are still trying to prove that you are somebody. That is a hard prison to live in.

Man: (Tears form in his eyes.) I guess I have proven that I'm not worth anything.

Therapist: I don't think so. I just think that you have proven that you can't do it by making money and working hard. When things were going well with you financially, you still wanted to be more. You would work harder. I think you have always been trying to prove your mother wrong. That you are somebody. But the hard-working part of you is not all of who you are. It is just the part of you that earns money.

Man: Then, what is the other part? Because all my life has been is work, work, work.

Therapist: I don't know yet. Tell me, what is it that your family could do that would make this bankruptcy easier for you?

Man: They wouldn't do it.

Therapist: I know they wouldn't right now, but what would you want?

Man: I wish they would just tell me that they appreciate what I've tried to do and tell me that we will get through this. (To the wife) You don't know how scary it is when all your life you have been able to work your way out of situations and you come to the place at the end of your life where you can't get out. (Wife stares coldly.)

Therapist: It is scary. So you want them to pull close?

Man: I know I haven't been a good husband or father, and I can't expect anything. It would be something.

Therapist: Now I think I may know a little more about you. You have been working so hard because you are frightened. Frightened that no one will see you as vulnerable and take care of you. So you work hard so you won't be vulnerable. Work keeps you away from feeling that fear. It has appeared to keep you safe emotionally. Just as it appeared to keep you safe from your mother swallowing you up. But I know that there is this part of you, that has always been a part of you, that needed to be accepted and told it was going to be okay. That's what your parents didn't give you that they should have. Maybe they didn't get it from their parents, but they still were responsible for giving it to you.

The man sat quietly for several minutes and then acknowledged that this was much of what he felt. For the rest of the session, the psychotherapist and the man spoke about this entitlement that he carried, which illustrated how his feelings and behaviors stemmed from his efforts to get relief. His wife was present during the entire session but was still very stoic. In the next session, the effort turned toward recognizing the inappropriateness of how he attempted to get relief in his family.

Inappropriate Claims on Innocent Parties. The man and his wife returned the next week, and the man articulated well a summary of the previous session, in which he confirmed that he indeed had always desired for someone to care for him, but that he covered this by work. The psychotherapist used this knowledge to focus the man on his responsibility for putting this claim on his family.

Therapist: (To the wife) Tell me, what is it that you have been denied in this marriage?

Woman: A husband. He has never been there for me and left me totally to raise the kids by myself. Whenever something went wrong at home, he would curse at me and tell me how incompetent I was. I finally learned to just leave him out of everything. It was easier.

Therapist: Was it this way when you first met?

Woman: I suppose. He was fun when we first met and I got a little swept away by him. I knew that he would be a good provider.

Therapist: Has he been a good provider?

Woman: Yes, until this recent blowup.

Therapist: (To the man) I know that you have been a good provider, but you carried the things that you got from your family right into the marriage. You still wanted everything to be okay. When you felt vulnerable, you would work to try and prove yourself.

Man: I suppose so.

Therapist: How do you think that affected your family? Tell me about how you think it affected each person.

Man: (Frequently pauses between sentences) Well, I know it has affected them all. My son, I know that he didn't know what to do, coming out of school, so he came to work with me. I wanted him to work with me, but I made him ask me. I was going to give the business to him, but I have never been able to let go. My other son, I don't know. My daughter, I suppose she thinks that she never had a father. That's probably right. We never had a relationship. My wife. It's just like she says. I was a provider, but I was never around. When something went wrong, I blamed her. I just didn't want to be bothered.

Therapist: (Long pause) So you wanted your family to be okay. You had an emotional need for them to be okay. But you were afraid you would get swallowed up like you did with your mother if you got emotionally involved. So you went away to work. When things didn't work at home, you blamed them because it made you feel unstable.

Man: That's exactly right.

Therapist: (To the wife) I don't really think your husband is going to get any better until he recognizes that what he has done with you and your children is wrong. It's not that he is totally to blame; after all, he really had some traumatic circumstances where he learned this game. But I know that it has taken a toll on you. (Wife softens and acknowledges the therapist being correct.)

Therapist: (To the man) You indeed were left out in the cold when you were a boy. You did an admirable job of trying to cope with a bad situation. You took care of yourself to calm your fears and the pain of what you didn't get from your parents. The problem is, you continued to do that as an adult. Your family needed from you what you needed from your parents. Instead . . .

Man: Instead they got someone who was never there and blamed them for mistakes.

Therapist: Yes. You need to have your needs addressed, but you can't do it by playing this out with your wife and children.

Man: What do I do?

Therapist: You have to acknowledge what you have done and stop putting them through this game that made you feel better.

Man: (To the wife) Do you want me to do that? (The wife doesn't answer.)

Therapist: Just try it and she will decide when she sees it.

Man: I understand that I have avoided you and what you needed.

I know how I have left you to manage things by yourself.
I'm in desperate need, but I want you to know that I will
try to do differently by you. I know I can't pay you back,
but I can do things differently.

At this point, the woman softened even more, and by the end of
the session, she told her husband, "We will get through this." This
was clear evidence that the meager resources that were present were
starting to build some trustworthiness with the couple. The next two
sessions were spent talking about specific actions that the man needed
to take with each of his three children, in order to communicate that
he had inappropriately forced his relational issues on them.

Getting Entitlement Appropriately Addressed. Many times, as
stated in the previous chapter, the entitlement of a patient can be
addressed by returning to the people who caused the violation of
love and trust in the first place. Also, using groups, reading, and
spiritual resources can be of help. In this case, however, the man's
parents were long since dead and he was not well connected to any
group. The psychotherapist decided that the best option available
was for the man to get used to expressing his desire to be cared for
and reassured and then moving to care for and reassure his wife and
children that he would not seek this from them. This proved to be a
trustworthy act and neutralized the distrust and hate that the children
and the wife had for the man. The man's depression lifted significantly as the therapy progressed, the financial situation and consequences became clearer, and the medication took effect.

The psychotherapist now turned his attention to transforming
the legacy of distrust and violation with the family group as a whole.
The man asked each of his children to attend therapy, "to help him
face the consequences of his actions." All three agreed to come.

Working Up and Working Down

As stated before, this technique is about the psychotherapist working
in a three-generational complex in order to address family ledger
issues (Hargrave & Metcalf, 2000). The flexibility of working up one
generation and down one generation gives the psychotherapist the
opportunity to avoid defensiveness and aggression among family
members. In particularly damaging families, the tendency toward defensiveness and aggression is high. The psychotherapist, while acknowledging and being partial to all members' ledger issues, is able

to avoid the defensiveness or aggressiveness by switching the generational focus of the person in stress. At the beginning of the seventh session, all three children, as well as the man and his wife, were present. The psychotherapist used the first part of the session to join with the children about their jobs and families, then moved to address the ledger issues.

Therapist: Your father, mother, and I have identified that your father grew up in a situation where he wasn't cared for emotionally, and emotions were used to get him to take responsibility. He learned to avoid these emotions by staying away and working. We have dealt with the ways that he carried this into your family. I want to hear from each one of you some of the effects of his behavior on you.

1st Son: I never have pleased him. He never looked at things I did or accomplished. He never has trusted me in the business. I've just learned to put up with him and avoid him. My mistake was not leaving a long time ago.

Daughter: (Crying) I've always wondered what was wrong with me that he wouldn't take notice of me. Nothing. Anything that he has ever said to me, especially since high school, has been criticism.

2nd Son: He was just never there. I learned real early that the best way to deal with him was avoid him totally.

Therapist: And how about your mother?

Daughter: (After the three look at one another.) Mom was really more of one of us. She just coped with him like the rest of us.

Therapist: (To the father) When you hear your children speak, what do you feel?

Father: (In a depressed and defensive tone.) I feel like everyone is ganging up on me.

1st Son: Well, I'm sorry, but you pretty much deserve it.

Therapist: Maybe so. (To the father) Tell me, how did you feel the day that your mother told you to leave home and not come back?

Man: I thought, "Fine. I will take care of myself." I thought that I just wouldn't have to deal with her.

Therapist: Did you feel any softness or tenderness toward her?

Man: No. I still don't.

Therapist: You see, your mother didn't give you much emotionally
            and instead expected you to pick up responsibilities to
            help her. You still don't have any warmth for her after all
            these years. This is what it's like for your children. You
            didn't give them much emotionally either and were hard
            on them.

Notice here that as soon as the man became defensive, it sparked
a harsh reaction from the son. Instead of responding to the harsher
statement, the psychotherapist went to where the defensiveness began
and helped the man recognize that his children were not doing anything
different from what he did with his mother. This fact enlightened the
father's understanding and softened his defensiveness as he responded.

Man: I know that what I have done to you kids through these
            years has been bad. I was just trying to be a good pro-
            vider, but I didn't give you kids any care.
1st Son: You still don't.
Daughter: Joc.
1st Son: You know that's true. He doesn't appreciate what we have
            done. He never has supported us. He made all of us work
            through college but never recognized our efforts. He doesn't
            even know all the names of his grandchildren. He doesn't
            recognize us, but his grandchildren are nonexistent.

The son had very justified anger, but the anger was destructive in
response to the father's effort to take some responsibility. The psychotherapist then shifted the generational perspective down.

Therapist: You have children. How many?
1st Son: I have two daughters. Ages 18 and 13.
Therapist: If they were here, what do you think they would say about
            your father?
1st Son: They would say he is nonexistent, too. They don't know
            anything about him.
Therapist: What do you suppose they would say about you?
1st Son: (A bit off guard) I think they would say I'm a good father.
            I'm not perfect. I work too much and worry too much. I'm
            a little hard on them.
Therapist: I am sure that you have done better than what was done

	for you. Tell me, have they ever told you that you work too much?
1st Son:	No. I know they think that, though, because of their mother. My wife tells me all the time. I think mothers and daughters are closer.
Therapist:	Little doubt. Are they close to you?
1st Son:	They know I love them.
Therapist:	If there is ever a day when they want to talk to you about working too much—better yet, if there ever is a day that you want to tell them that you didn't spend enough time with them when they were little, how would you like them to respond?
1st Son:	Okay, I get the point. I am too angry and I should be more open.
Therapist:	No, my point is different. My point is that what we do here will have a direct bearing on you being able to be honest and direct with your children. I want to try and get some issues settled for you and your father, but I want to make absolutely sure that you will be able to settle issues with your daughters.

With this, very constructive dialogue opened up about what the children missed from their father. This was done with only a minimum amount of defensiveness. The technique of working up and working down consistently reminds the family members that they are not only in the position of being entitled in ledger issues; they are also in the position of being obligated. This specifically allows the family members to more easily take responsibility for actions and be more hesitant to pursue destructive actions.

The session ended with no dramatic changes in the family, but the responsibility taken by the father and the recognition of the children's responsibilities diffused the anger enough in the family that meeting again was a possibility. Although this was a small step, it was nonetheless a trustworthy effort that mobilized enough resources in the family to see some hopefulness in continuing the dialogue.

Balancing Obligations and Entitlements

With this technique, the primary idea is to move the family members past the long-standing ledger imbalance on which relationships have been judged and to initiate specific opportunities for addressing obligations and entitlements. This technique was first identified by Hargrave and Anderson (1992) in connection with their work with older families. It was noticed that with many older families, the aging member was often removed from the opportunity to contribute to the family in effective or meaningful ways. As a result, the ledger imbalance would prompt many aging members to feel guilty and perhaps become depressed, angry, and rejecting because they did not want the family to do anything more for them, or hopeless because they were unable to give anything meaningful to the family.

The same conditions exist in any family complex. When there is damage or dysfunction, family members often stop interacting at all. In essence, the old damage or ledger imbalances harden like concrete. As mentioned before, this creates an emotional field in the family that is seldom based in the present but instead is based on the "mythology" of the past. In these situations, one can articulate specific obligations and entitlements that belong to the relational ledger of the family. Of course, articulating *some* of what makes up the injustices or imbalances in the family does not mean that we can understand *all* of what exists in the dimension of relational ethics or even any one particular relational ledger between individuals. However, it is important that we point out specifics where giving and taking in relationships can start in the present. As family members give to one another, they earn merit or entitlement in the present. As this merit and entitlement are satisfied, noticeable and specific steps are taken in building trustworthiness. Trustworthiness, in turn, stimulates family members to give more to others (Boszormenyi-Nagy & Krasner, 1986).

In this particular family, the distrust was high and energy was very low toward making changes. Direct giving can sometimes be too threatening. The man had spent 43 years damaging his family. As members of his family saw it, he had a turn of bad luck and was now in need of something from them. They did not trust that he was really confronting his past and taking responsibility for his actions. The psychotherapist, therefore, decided on a tact of indirect giving through the grandchildren. All family members were once again present at the eighth session.

Therapist: I have thought much about all of you this past week. I was particularly thinking about something that one of you said about your father. You said that he did not know the names of his grandchildren. (Several nods from the daughter and 1st son) I haven't been able to sort through every-thing in terms of what I want your father to start doing in the family, but clearly, I think that he needs to start taking his responsibility as a grandfather. What sort of things would be acceptable for your father to do for your children?

Daughter: My son really doesn't know Dad. I'm not sure he would really want to spend any time with him. He would have to be asked.

Therapist: I want to be clear. It might not be just spending time. Are there things that they need? Help he can give them? Things he can teach? Anything at all?

Daughter: (Thinks for a moment and says to the father.) If you really wanted to get his attention, do something with cars or trucks. He is at that stage where he wants his own truck. He loves to think about vehicles and work on them.

Therapist: This is a good idea. (To the father) Do you have an interest in starting a relationship with your grandchildren?

Man: Yes, but I can't buy him a truck.

Therapist: I know that's the case, but you have to think about what would be good for him. If you were 16 and not on your own, you loved vehicles but didn't have one of your own, what would you want or need?

Man: I guess I would want a vehicle. I might try to get some-thing on my own.

Daughter: You don't have to get him a truck. Just teach him how to drive or teach him how to work on trucks. You are good at that.

Man: Would he do it?

Daughter: I don't know. You would have to ask him yourself.

Here the daughter provided the father with an opportunity to get to know her son. The man did not demonstrate any ability to think about what was good for others because it was very far from his lifetime orientation. The therapist explored the idea of teaching the son to drive with the man, and the daughter gave him information about the son. Instead of sending him home with the objective of calling his grandson, the psychotherapist suggested that he make the call during the session. The daughter coached the father on what he could say to her son that would be a good approach, and the father called his grandson. Although small, this was further evidence that the daughter was willing to use her resources of giving to stimulate the trustworthy effort in the family. After the call, the first son joined in the conversation about what his father could do for his children.

Man: I'll be damned. He said that would be great.

Daughter: All you have to do is ask, Dad.

1st Son: I've been thinking all this time of what you could do for my girls.

Therapist: Have you come up with anything?

1st Son: I have trouble imagining that they would want to spend any time with you because I don't want to spend any time with you. I'm not trying to be mean, it is just that no one knows you.

Man: (Exasperated) All I can tell you is that I am willing to try. I'm not good at this stuff and you know it. But I am willing to try.

1st Son: I'm not trying to make you mad, I was just thinking about maybe you could buy them something, but I know that you are in the same financial mess that I'm in. I thought maybe you could give them something from the house that might be meaningful.

Man: Like what?

1st Son: I really don't want to say. I just was trying to give you an idea.

This was a very positive sign in the therapy because it demonstrated that there was an escalating effort toward giving in the family. It also marked the first time that the eldest son did not respond to the father in a defensive way when the father responded defensively. This was a strong act of extension on the son's part that indicated further willingness to engage. The psychotherapist suggested that the father think about what he could give from his possessions that might be meaningful to his son's daughters.

On the ninth session, the second son did not attend. This was one of the strong risks that the psychotherapist took by initiating giving to grandchildren, in that the second son had no children. The time that the man spent with his grandson, however, was very successful. The man took the boy out driving not only once but three times to give him more learning time. The daughter was pleased. However, the father did not come up with anything to give his granddaughters.

The psychotherapist anticipated this as a possibility and utilized it as a further opportunity for giving in the family.

Therapist: (To the woman) Tell me, are you very good at reading your granddaughters?

Woman: Well, I'm more involved than he is, but I don't know them well.

Therapist: I'm wondering if you could perhaps help him and join in on identifying something that would be meaningful to them?

Woman: (Looks at the man tentatively.) I think I could do that.

For the next session, the psychotherapist made a call to connect with the second son, to say that he was now intending to suggest that the father give directly to his kids. The son had only tentative interest but agreed to attend the next session, and he did. The man and the woman did work together, and they gave their granddaughters each a rocking chair that they had had in their houses for years. The first son reported that the daughters were surprised by the gifts and made comments to him about how that was not like his parents. They asked him several more questions about his parents.

1st Son: It was good. They asked some really tough questions about why you two haven't been around much like other grand-parents. I didn't make excuses for you, but I realized that I was saying things to them that were explanations instead of accusations. So, really, I think you giving the chairs to them was helpful to me.

Woman: It was helpful for me, too. I think that this was the first time in years that we did something as husband and wife. I know this is terrible to think that doing something as normal as seeing your granddaughters is an achievement, but for us it is.

Therapist: How was it helpful?

Woman: I just thought that we maybe could do this.

The giving had the desired effect, and the family members now became more open to engaging in the relationships. The giving had also helped significantly with the man's depression. During the week, he had also taken his grandson driving again, and they stopped at a drive-in for lunch. The psychotherapist then turned the conversation toward direct giving, by asking each one of the children what they could use from their parents.

1st Son:	Well, involvement with my girls is a help. (Pause) To tell you the truth, Dad, I need your help down at the office. You have run the thing for so many years without letting me make decisions or know what is going on, now I'm trying to clean up this mess.
Man:	I just don't know if I can go back down there. I feel so hopeless anytime I think about the business. (1st son shrugs his shoulders.)
Therapist:	It is a risk. It may cause you to go back into depression. But your son is asking for something specific.
1st Son:	Forget it. I don't want to put pressure on you. I don't really want you to get back involved either because you might try and take the thing over again.

This was an important moment in the therapy. In many ways, work and money had been what the father was always about. Now, it was the source of great depression. To go back to work would be a clear demonstration of the father's willingness to give to the son. For the son, however, the offer was a great risk because the father had abused him as an employee, instead of letting him take over the business.

Therapist:	I am a little hesitant to forget it. (Looking at the 2nd son.) What do you think?
2nd Son:	Me? I don't think about that thing. I had to work there to get through college, but I have no desire to know anything about it. I don't want to know.
Therapist:	I realize that it is a source of pain, but what if you could stay outside and just look at it from a business perspective? Would that be possible?
2nd Son:	Sure. But I'm not going to solve any problems. This is their business, not mine.
Therapist:	That sounds good. (Looking at the father) Could you take the material to your son's office and all three of you talk about it there?
Man:	I'll give it a try.
Therapist:	(To the 1st son) Would that be helpful?
1st Son:	We could give it a try.

The three met at night at the second son's office for 5 hours. The psychotherapist's intention of involving the second son was to initiate some opportunity for the father to respect his abilities. The second son, however, proved to be invaluable. The man indeed had made some huge financial mistakes through the years but always managed to keep the business going. The first son's anger grew, and the father became defensive. The second son, however, was the one who kept them on track and encouraged a very pragmatic problem-solving style. The result was that the second son discovered some assets that the father had inadvertently moved that were protected from the proceedings. Although the amount was not great, it was substantial enough to care for the first son's needs for several months. The second son confronted the father directly, saying, "Joe has put in all this time when he should have had this business 10 years ago. It's none of my business, but as your son, I think that it is time you put your money where your mouth is and give all the money to him." The man's tendency was to move back in and take control of the money himself. This was a distinct possibility for him, especially because his depression had abated. Although it was difficult for him, he did agree that the money should go to his first son, and he eventually apologized for the poor decisions he had made with the business. This was all revealed in the 11th session.

Within the course of 5 weeks, the family direction had changed significantly. All family members were actively speaking and had demonstrated giving in the present. The man had much to make up for with his wife and children. All reported having moments and days when they still resented the man for things that he had done. The daughter also began to express that she had been angry with the mother for "checking out" all those years when she was in need. These problems are very common to the contextual therapy process, as family members confront old wounds and behaviors. But the entire family acknowledged that there had been significant progress made toward things getting better. Primarily, the man's wife and children actually believed that he was trying to make a difference in the family. Essentially, this is what the technique of balancing obligations and entitlements is about. It stimulates giving to build trustworthiness. This trust builds possibilities and hope, which have the power to transform old patterns and beliefs.

Salvage, Restoration, and Blessing

Contextual therapy has a concept that is called *exoneration*. Exoneration is the idea of lifting the load of culpability off a person who has previously been blamed for a violation. Boszormenyi-Nagy and Krasner

(1986) believe that exoneration differs from forgiveness, in that exoneration does not retain the assumption of guilt of the blamed party. Forgiveness, on the other hand, retains the concept of guilt, yet the forgiver forgoes the need to punish the guilty party. Although many would agree with this concept of forgiveness, we do not. We believe that exoneration and forgiveness can and do meld. Forgiveness is the process by which love and trust are reestablished in relationships (Hargrave, 2001). In order to reestablish love and trust, the concept of justice and balance are absolutely essential. This obligation toward justice makes responsibility a requirement of balanced relationships. Responsibility, then, requires that we acknowledge that irresponsibility or violations of justice took place. Guilt, in our view, is not so much something a person feels, as it is something that is done. Acknowledgment of guilt, therefore, is not a bad thing. Indeed, to acknowledge guilt is to make a move toward establishing justice. Exoneration is good, in that it lifts the load of culpability off someone whom we blamed for violations. Doing so means that we see that and acknowledge that this person was also subject to a legacy and a ledger of violations that contributed to the irresponsible behavior. Forgiveness, however, holds violators and the violated accountable to make loving and trustworthy behavior in the future. Forgiveness replaces guilt with the possibility of giving and replaces punishment with responsible commitment to do no further damage.

We have detailed the work of forgiveness from this contextual perspective in other works (Hargrave, 1994, 2001; Hargrave & Anderson, 1992). The work of forgiveness fits into two broad categories: *salvage* and *restoration.* Salvage is the use of forgiveness to gain insight into how to keep the damage done in the past from continuing to affect one's life now and in the future. It also means understanding the circumstances of the abused, so that one does not carry the burden of pain alone. The concepts of understanding described in the previous chapter are sufficient to explain how processing the development, circumstances, and limitations of a person who caused a violation can effect change in an individual's sense of self and thereby change the way he or she interacts with others. The work of salvage assumes that the relationship itself may be too damaged or may be too unloving or trustworthy to reengage. The work of salvage, however, essentially allows a person who has experienced violations to form some sense of exoneration of the violator and to move past the violation's effects to do good in other relationships. Salvage, in other words, does not restore love and trust to the damaged relationship, but it does help ensure their presence in future relationships (Hargrave, 2001).

Restoration is different from salvage, in that it requires the person who suffered the violation to move back into the very relationship that caused the violation. Restoration means that the victim and the victimizer work together to restore love and trust and to make the relationship functional again. This work of forgiveness is accomplished by the victim allowing the victimizer to rebuild trustworthiness and love in a sequential fashion, called giving the opportunity for compensation or overt forgiving, which is overtly confronting the past violations and seeking forgiveness (Hargrave, 2001). The previous discussion on balancing obligations and entitlements is very similar to giving the opportunity for compensation. The man's children allowed the father to demonstrate some trustworthy action by giving to the grandchildren. Because that effort was successful, the children were willing to trust the father to give more directly to them. This is basically how trust and love are rebuilt by giving the opportunity for compensation, and restoration of the relationship is established. Restoration by overt forgiving will be discussed later in this chapter.

Therefore, the work of forgiveness is divided into the two broad categories of *salvage* and *restoration*. Salvage has two stations, *insight* and *understanding*. Restoration has two stations of *giving the opportunity for compensation* and *overt forgiving*. A diagram illustrating the work of forgiveness is found in table 7.1. It is important to note that even though the work of forgiveness is the goal of both salvage and restoration, the two are very different and are appropriate in different relationships at different times. Also important to note is that there are four stations in the work of forgiveness. These should not be interpreted as *stages*, in that one precedes or follows another. The stations are intertwined, but one cannot assume that forgiveness moves from one station to the next. Rather, people who work at forgiving usually oscillate among these stations many times, in the course of trying to heal violations from the past (Hargrave, 2001).

When family members go about the work of forgiveness and especially of restoration, they are making intentional efforts to transform what was once damaging and crippling to the relational ethic of

TABLE 7.1
The Four Stations of Forgiveness

THE WORK OF FORGIVENESS			
Salvage		Restoration	
Insight	Understanding	Giving the Opportunity for Compensation	Overt Forgiving

future generations and strengthening it so as to heal dysfunction and make healthier individuals. As stated before, this effort is both loving and trustworthy and has transcendent effects that far outlast the people who make the effort. As such, the process of restoration carries the possibility of actually blessing the future.

In the previous case, the psychotherapist saw much progress and promise with the increasing levels of trustworthiness in the family. The father's actions with the first son, particularly with regard to the money and the business, improved their relationship dramatically. Although this was encouraging, the first son rightly pointed out that "It's going to take a while before we are okay, but we are certainly better." This was an indication that he was willing to pursue a tact of giving the opportunity for compensation with regard to restoration. The second son had yet to make any clear commitment toward letting the father engage in direct giving. Most likely, of the three children he was the one most similar to the father and found ways to escape when he felt emotionally vulnerable. He was, however, clearly engaged into the family process by his actions with his father and his brother. This engagement to help was, at minimum, a willingness to see how the family progressed. The wife and the daughter, on the other hand, were looking for something deeper from the father. Although they acknowledged that the father was trying, they would have much difficulty around specific things he had done, said, or failed to do in the past. For this reason, the psychotherapist thought that overt forgiving would be appropriate.

Hargrave (2001) pointed out that overt forgiving is like a point of demarcation that can serve as a new beginning in a relationship, which separates the individuals from the violations of the past. There are three aspects to be accomplished in this overt forgiving process. These are: (1) agreement upon the violation that was done; (2) acknowledgment of the violation and the taking of responsibility; and (3) apology, which serves as a promise to live in loving and trustworthy ways in the future. Before the 12th session, the psychotherapist contacted the man, the woman, and the daughter concerning their willingness to participate in an overt forgiving session. All were willing to try. The two brothers were informed of the plan just before the session and were invited to participate, observe, or not attend if they did not feel comfortable. Both decided to stay. The session began with the psychotherapist exploring the possibility of agreement. This involved identifying the "heart of the violation."

Therapist: (To the woman) I know that this is difficult because you have felt abandoned and abused by your husband in many

	ways. But it would be helpful if you could name the heart of what he has done to you.
Woman:	I don't know if I can do that.
Therapist:	I know that it is difficult to do. (Turns to the daughter) Is it possible for you to do it?
Daughter:	I think so. He was never really interested in me. I remember, as a little girl, coming to him with a drawing or wanting to sit beside him to watch television. He would literally just get up and leave. I think that I have spent a good part of my life looking for a daddy. I think I had this fantasy that when I got involved with drugs, mom or dad would step in and save me. When that didn't work, I got pregnant to say, "Hey, I'm over here." They still wouldn't get involved. They would give me a little money and send me along. I remember one note that Dad dropped off at my apartment when my son was a baby. It had $400 in an envelope and a note with five words. "I am ashamed of you." For me, that's the heart of it.
Man:	(Defensive) I don't remember that.
Daughter:	(Defensive) Well, you sure did it.
Therapist:	Hold on for a minute. Remember, we are here to be constructive, so it is important for me to keep us on track. (Looking at the man) It really isn't that important whether or not you remember that specific incident. What your daughter is telling you is that she went through life believing that you were not interested in her. She has felt that either you were indifferent to her, you were ashamed of her, or you disliked her. (Now looking at the daughter) Do I have that correct?
Daughter:	Yes. That's it.
Therapist:	(To the woman) Have you had enough time to think?
Woman:	I think, for me, it is a little of the same. Except my problem with him has always been that we were never a priority with him. He never gave me the time of day for all those years, yet he would expect me to orbit around him like that was my only concern. Any time that I would get out of line, he would come down on me like a hammer. Those are the things that made me sick. After about 5 years of marriage, I just emotionally went away.
Therapist:	That is understandable. Do you still feel away?

Woman: I feel better. But it really only takes a minute for me to go right back to that distance when I think about anything.

Therapist: So the heart of it for you is that he made you no priority at all, while he expected you to live your life around him. When you didn't, he attacked you and said terrible things to you.

Woman: I think that it's a little more than that. I think it's that he made me go away. I don't like who I am any more than I like him.

Therapist: That is most helpful. (To the man) You've heard what they have to say. Are these things true about you? Did you act like your daughter didn't mean anything to you? Did you treat your wife so unfairly that it drove her right out of being emotionally connected?

Man: I suppose so.

Therapist: If you didn't, tell me because I want to hear your side of the story. But if it is true, I need you to say so.

Man: It's true. (Looking at the daughter) It was certainly not that I didn't like you. I was too involved with other things to pay attention to you. Until recently, I really thought that the world should orbit around my work—around me doing my work. I felt like you should be more responsible.

Therapist: Are you saying that some of this was her fault?

Man: No. I was thinking that she needed to be like me. That would be a good reflection on me. I was a good parent if my children were responsible and hard-working. (Looking at his daughter) There were times that I was ashamed of you, but that was because of me. I mostly just never thought about you.

Therapist: And what about what your wife said?

Man: I think that is exactly what I did. She is a good woman. My thought was that as a wife, she should just shut up and keep the home and kids on track. I did and said some horrible things. (Pauses) I know what she is talking about when she says that she went away. I remember when it happened. I just stood by and let it happen and pretended like she was the problem.

Agreement is not always this easy to accomplish. There are many times when people want to talk about specific incident after specific incident. As this happens, the likelihood of defensiveness increases. Most violations, however, have a common theme. It is important for the psychotherapist to keep the individuals focused on the overall violation, to not get off track. In this case, the agreement on the heart of violation was reached quickly. The mother and daughter, however, needed several conversations about the father's feelings and knowledge of the violations. This is often the case. In most cases where an overt forgiving is planned for a session, reaching and exploring agreement may last 40 to 50 minutes.

About 45 minutes into the session, the psychotherapist turned the family toward the process of acknowledgment. This is most likely the key element in overt forgiveness, because the victimized party has been committed to holding the victimizer responsible for his or her unloving and untrustworthy actions. Restoration will demand that the victim release that desire to hold the victimizer responsible. This can be achieved, in our opinion, only when the victimizer holds himself or herself responsible for the violation. The victim no longer has any need to hold the victimizer responsible because the victimizer holds the responsibility (Hargrave, 2001).

Because this is such a critical point in the therapy, it is helpful to make the memory of this event more intense. This can be accomplished through the use of rituals. Rituals can be helpful because they intensify the elements of change that the therapeutic process is encouraging. This, in turn, makes the effort at transformation easier. Other advantages are: (1) Rituals serve as anchors in the memory of the family or the couple; (2) Performing a ritual is very hard to do if you really do not mean what the ritual represents; and (3) They access second-order emotions in the field of relational ethics. The violator getting on his or her knees is a common ritual used by Hargrave (1994), based on previous work by Madanes. Others include burning representations of the violation, extinguishing candles that represent pain, and burying a jar filled with notes of the terrible emotions that resulted from the violation. The use of rituals requires a good working alliance, and the rituals have to be adapted to the family, its cultural and religious background. In this particular case, the psychotherapist decided to use a heavy stone as part of the ritual to effect both acknowledgment and apology.

Therapist: (To the man) I believe you really understand now the impact that your irresponsibility has had on your marriage and your daughter. They have been carrying around this burden of neglect and emotional withdrawal for many years. (Gets out of his chair and places large stones in the laps of the woman and daughter.) In carrying around that burden, your daughter has tried to get your attention by creating problems in her life. But you still left her to carry the burden. Your wife has had to lug around this burden for 43 years and, as a result, found that the only way she could handle it was to act like it didn't hurt. She went away emotionally. They carry these burdens because of the burden you carry from your family. But you have passed it along to them. What do you want to do?

Man: I don't want them to carry it anymore.

Therapist: Then you must take the burden off them by acknowledging full responsibility for the damage they have had to bear and must take it on yourself.

Man: (Tears fill his eyes and he looks at the floor.) I have treated you wrong and did exactly what you said. (To the daughter) I neglected you and put work ahead of you and made you feel like you didn't even matter to me. (To the woman) I never made you a priority in my life and treated you so badly, you went away and closed your heart. (Tears stream from his face as he looks up.)

Therapist: Now I think that you are ready to take this burden off them. (Removes both of the stones and places them on the man's lap.)

Therapist: (Long pause, and then looking at the woman and the daughter.) He says that he wants to take responsibility for the burdens that he has placed on both of you. Do you believe he means it?

Daughter: I think he finally means it.

Woman: I think that I can believe him. I think I can believe him more.

Therapist: Then what do you want him to do with these burdens?

Woman: What do you mean?

Therapist: If you want him to, I will have him sit in a chair once a day for an hour with these stones on his lap and think about the pain that he has caused the two of you.

Daughter: I don't want him to do that. (Woman shakes her head.)

Therapist: Then what do you want him to do with these burdens?

2nd Son: Throw the damn things out the window! (Everyone laughs.)

Daughter: Yeah, throw the damn things out the window. (Therapist looks to the woman.)

Woman: I think that's as good as anything.

Therapist: Good. But just before you get rid of these burdens, it's necessary to apologize. Apology is not so much saying you are sorry, as it is saying that if you had the chance to do it again, you would change. And that you will live differently from here on out.

Man: (Pauses, then says to his wife and daughter.) I have wasted a life. But I'm not going to waste any more time. I'm not perfect, but I promise the two of you that I will not forget to live differently.

After the man made his statement, the psychotherapist opened the window. The daughter and the father threw the heavy stones out the window of the two-story house and sent them crashing below. The family laughed, and then the man embraced his daughter first, then his wife.

Of course, restoration is not perfect. This family had made substantial progress but had difficult tasks to negotiate as the daughter went back to school, the son and the father dealt with legal and financial difficulties, and the husband and the wife struggled to emotionally reconnect. But neither was the family the same. The man was much more focused on making his wife a priority and made it a point to have lunch with each of his children every 2 weeks. He took a special interest in his daughter's son and eventually gave the boy his own truck. The family did not come in again after the 12th session, and the man and the woman continued marital therapy for 4 more sessions. They had accomplished the heart of transformation, which was turning the old wounds and violations of love and trust into new possibilities of connecting, nurturing, and living responsibly.

Final Thoughts on Contextual Therapy

Contextual therapy has the potential to transform painful violations into healthier relationships and individuals. We do almost all of our work from individual or family therapy, but we also believe that love, trust, and responsibility are essential for living as a global community. Our world has been brought together much more closely by communication and transportation, yet we fracture more severely on issues of national, racial, ethnic, and economic differences. We all have pasts and ledger issues that pertain not only to family but also to our relationships to the wider systemic framework of the world.

Contextual therapy is not only a therapy; it is also a philosophy, one that recognizes that justice must have due consideration in all relationships. One that recognizes that violations, though inevitable, are never justified. One that is partial to the interests of people as individuals, as well as to the interests of the couple, the family, and society as a whole. One that maintains a position of hopefulness that even in conditions of extreme violation and pain, resources and strengths are present and can be used to increase justice, peace, and love.

Contextual therapy needs to be well understood and practiced because it is one of the methodologies that offers real solutions to both the family and the global community. It is not that these solutions are easily found or easily practiced. But the solutions and transformations that contextual therapy offers do present humans with a clear opportunity to understand themselves better and to live in trustworthy ways. As such, it is our hope that contextual therapy will be practiced not only as a therapy but as a way of diplomacy and negotiation. In a world that has become as fractured and destructive as ours, we will likely depend on these elements to survive.

References

Ainsworth, M. D. S., & Bowlby, J. (1991). An ethological approach to personality development. *American Psychologist, 46,* 331–341.

Aggleton, J. P. (Ed.). (1992). *The amygdala: Neurobiological aspects of emotion, memory, and mental dysfunction.* New York: Wiley-Liss.

Amato, P. R., & Booth, A. (1997). *A generation at risk: Growing up in an era of family upheaval.* Cambridge, MA: Harvard University Press.

Antonowsky, A. (1984). A call or a new question—salutogenesis—and a proposed answer. *Journal of Professional Psychiatry, 1,* 1–13.

Baltimore, D. (2001). Our human genome unveiled. *Nature, 409,* 814–816.

Boszormenyi-Nagy, I., Grunebaum, J., & Ulrich, D. (1991). Contextual therapy. In A. S. Gurman & D. P. Kniskern (Eds.), *Handbook of family therapy* (Vol. II). New York: Brunner/Mazel.

Boszormenyi-Nagy, I., & Krasner, B. (1986). *Between give and take: A clinical guide to contextual therapy.* New York: Brunner/Mazel.

Boszormenyi-Nagy, I., & Spark, G. (1984). *Invisible loyalties.* New York: Brunner/Mazel.

Boszormenyi-Nagy, I., & Ulrich, D. N. (1981). Contextual family therapy. In A. S. Gurman & D. P. Kniskern (Eds.), *Handbook of family therapy* (pp. 159–186). New York: Brunner/Mazel.

Buber, M. (1958). *I and thou.* New York: Charles Scribner & Sons.

Chomsky, N. (1972). *Language and mind.* New York: Harcourt Brace Jovanovich.

Cannon, W. B. (1932). *The wisdom of the body.* New York: Norton.

Coll, C. T. G. (1990). Developmental outcome of minority infants: A process-oriented look into our beginnings. *Child Development, 61,* 270–289.

Cotroneo, M., & Krasner, B. R. (1977). Abortion and problems in decision making. *Journal of Marriage and Family Counseling, 18,* 41–62.

Davies, C. T., & Cummings, E. M. (1998). Exploring children's emotional security as a mediator of the link between marital relations and child adjustment. *Child Development, 69,* 124–139.

deShazer, S. (1985). *Keys to solutions in brief therapy.* New York: Norton.

deShazer, S. (1991). *Putting differences to work.* New York: Norton.

Doherty, W. J. (1996). *Soul searching: Why psychotherapy must promote moral responsibility*. New York: Basic Books.

Erikson, E. H. (1963). *Childhood and society* (2nd ed.). New York: Norton & Company.

Fairbairn, W. R. (1963). Synopsis of an object relations theory of personality. *International Journal of Psychoanalysis, 44*, 224.

Goldenberg, I., & Goldenberg, H. (2000). *Family therapy: An overview* (5th ed.). Belmont, CA: Brooks/Cole.

Goldenthal, P. (1996). *Doing contextual therapy: An integrated model for working with individuals, couples, and families*. New York: Norton.

Grunebaum, J. (1997). Thinking about romantic/erotic love. *Journal of Marital and Family Therapy, 23*(3), 295–307.

Gurman, A. S., & Kniskern, D. P. (1981). Editor's note. In A. S. Gurman & D. P. Kniskern (Eds.), *Handbook of family therapy* (p. 185). New York: Brunner/Mazel.

Haley, J. (1987). *Problem solving therapy* (2nd ed.). San Francisco: Jossey-Bass.

Hargrave, T. D. (1994). *Families and forgiveness: Healing wounds in the intergenerational family*. New York: Brunner/Mazel.

Hargrave, T. D. (2000). *The essential humility of marriage: Honoring the third identity in couple therapy*. Phoenix, AZ: Zeig, Tucker & Theisen.

Hargrave, T. D. (2001). *Forgiving the devil: Coming to terms with damaged relationships*. Phoenix, AZ: Zeig, Tucker & Theisen.

Hargrave, T. D., & Anderson, W. T. (1992). *Finishing well: Aging and reparation in the intergenerational family*. New York: Brunner/Mazel.

Hargrave, T. D., Jennings, G., & Anderson, W. T. (1991). The development of a relational ethics scale. *Journal of Marital and Family Therapy, 17*, 145–159.

Hargrave, T. D., & Metcalf, L. (2000). Solution focused family of origin therapy. In L. VandeCreek & T. L. Jackson (Eds.), *Innovations in clinical practice: A source book* (Vol. 18; pp. 47–56). Sarasota, FL: Professional Resource Press.

Himelstein, S., Graham, S., & Weinter, B. (1991). An attributional analysis of maternal beliefs about the importance of child-rearing practices. *Child Development, 62*, 301–310.

Hockenbury, D. H., & Hockenbury, S. E. (2000). *Psychology* (2nd ed.). New York: Worth.

Human Genome Program. (2001). *Genomics and its impact on medicine and society: A 2001 primer*. Washington, DC: U.S. Department of Energy.

Jellouschek, H. (1998). *Wie partnerschaft gelingt: Spielregeln der liebe*. Freiburg, Germany: Herder.

LeDoux, J. E. (1994, June). Emotion, memory, and the brain. *Scientific American, 270*, 50–57.

LeDoux, J. E. (1996). *The emotional brain: The mysterious underpinnings of emotional life*. New York: Touchstone.

Li, W., Gu, Z., Wang, H., & Nekrutenko, A. (2001). Evolutionary analysis of the human genome. *Nature, 409*, 847–849.

Lieberman, A. F., Weston, D. R., & Prawl, J. H. (1991). Preventive intervention and outcome with anxiously attached dyads. *Child Development, 62*, 199–209.

Madanes, C. (1981). *Strategic family therapy.* San Francisco: Jossey-Bass.

Madanes, C. (1984). *Behind the one way mirror.* San Francisco: Jossey-Bass.

Minuchin, S. (1974). *Families and family therapy.* Cambridge, MA: Harvard University Press.

Minuchin, S., & Fishman, H. C. (1981). *Family therapy techniques.* Cambridge, MA: Harvard University Press.

Olds, J. (1958). Self stimulation of the brain. *Science, 127,* 315–324.

Pelaez-Nogueras, M., Gerwirtz, J. L., Field, T., Cigales, M., Malthurs, J., Clasky, S., & Sanchez, A. (1996). Infants' preference for touch stimulations in face to face interactions. *Journal of Applied Developmental Psychology, 67,* 1780–1792.

Pedersen, P. (1990). The multicultural perspective as a fourth force in counseling. *Journal of Mental Health Counseling, 12*(1), 93–95.

Pipp, S., Easterbrooks, M. A., & Harmon, R. J. (1992). The relation between attachment and knowledge of self and mother in one to three year old infants. *Child Development, 63,* 738–750.

Pipp, S., & Harmon, R. J. (1987). Attachment as regulation: A commentary. *Child Development, 58,* 648–652.

Prescott, C. A., & Gottesman, I. I. (1993). Genetically medicated vulnerability to schizophrenia. *Psychiatric Clinics of North America, 16,* 245–268.

Reiss, D. (1981). *The family's construction of reality.* Cambridge, MA: Harvard University Press.

Rice, F. P. (2000). *Human development* (4th ed.). Upper Saddle River, NJ: Prentice Hall.

Rogers, C. (1961). *On becoming a person.* Boston: Houghton Mifflin.

Saxton, L. (1993). *The individual, marriage, and the family* (8th ed.). Belmont, CA: Wadsworth.

Selvini-Palazzoli, M., Boscolo, L., Cecchin, G., & Prata, G. (1978). *Paradox and counterparadox: A new model in the therapy of the family in schizophrenic transaction.* New York: Aronson.

Sue, D. W., Ivey, A. E., & Pedersen, P. B. (1996). *A theory of multicultural counseling and therapy.* Pacific Grove, CA: Brooks/Cole.

Torgersen, S. (1990). Genetics of anxiety and its clinical implications. In G. D. Burrows, M. Roth, & R. Noyes (Eds.), *Handbook of anxiety: Vol. 3. The neurobiology of anxiety.* Amsterdam: Elsevier.

Tsuang, M. T., & Faraone, S. V. (1990). *The genetics of mood disorders.* Baltimore, MD: Johns Hopkins University Press.

Valenzuela, M. (1990). Attachment in chronically underweight young children. *Child Development, 61,* 1984–1996.

Van Heusden, A., & Van Den Eerenbeemt, E. (1987). *Balance in motion.* New York: Brunner/Mazel.

Watzlawick, P. (1967). *Pragmatics of human communication: A study of interactional patterns, pathologies, and paradoxes.* New York: Norton.

White, M. (1995). *Re-authoring lives: Interviews and essays.* Adelaide, South Australia: Dulwich Centre Publications.

Index

Anger + Hurt

Disrespect — men
Problem of doing

|

Unloving — women
Problem of being.